Maths

Assessment Papers

Up to Speed

10-11+ years

Great Clarendon Street, Oxford, OX2 6DP, United Kingdom

Oxford University Press is a department of the University of Oxford. It furthers the University's objective of excellence in research, scholarship, and education by publishing worldwide. Oxford is a registered trade mark of Oxford University Press in the UK and in certain other countries

Text © Paul Broadbent 2015
Illustrations © Oxford University Press 2015

The moral rights of the authors have been asserted

First published in 2015
This edition published in 2022

All rights reserved. No part of this publication may be reproduced, stored in a retrieval system, or transmitted, in any form or by any means, without the prior permission in writing of Oxford University Press, or as expressly permitted by law, by licence or under terms agreed with the appropriate reprographics rights organization. Enquiries concerning reproduction outside the scope of the above should be sent to the Rights Department, Oxford University Press, at the address above.

You must not circulate this work in any other form and you must impose this same condition on any acquirer

British Library Cataloguing in Publication Data
Data available

978-0-19-278507-7

10 9 8 7 6 5 4 3

Paper used in the production of this book is a natural, recyclable product made from wood grown in sustainable forests.
The manufacturing process conforms to the environmental regulations of the country of origin.

Printed in Great Britain by Ashford Colour Ltd

Acknowledgements

The publishers would like to thank the following for permissions to use copyright material:

Page make-up: GreenGate Publishing Services, Tonbridge, Kent
Cover illustrations: Lo Cole

Although we have made every effort to trace and contact all copyright holders before publication this has not been possible in all cases. If notified, the publisher will rectify any errors or omissions at the earliest opportunity.

Links to third party websites are provided by Oxford in good faith and for information only. Oxford disclaims any responsibility for the materials contained in any third party website referenced in this work.

The manufacturer's authorised representative in the EU for product safety is Oxford University Press España S.A. of El Parque Empresarial San Fernando de Henares, Avenida de Castilla, 2 – 28830 Madrid (www.oup.es/en or product.safety@oup.com). OUP España S.A. also acts as importer into Spain of products made by the manufacturer.

Introduction

What is Bond?

The Bond *Up to Speed* titles are part of the Bond range of assessment papers, the number one series for the 11+, selective exams and general practice. Bond *Up to Speed* is carefully designed to support children who need less challenging activities than those in the regular age-appropriate Bond papers, in order to build up and improve their techniques and confidence.

How does this book work?

The book contains two distinct sets of papers, along with full answers and a Progress Chart:

- Focus tests, accompanied by advice and directions, are focused on particular (and age-appropriate) maths question types encountered in the 11+ and other exams. The questions are deliberately set at a less challenging level than the standard *Assessment Papers*. Each Focus test is designed to help a child 'catch' their level in a particular question type, and then gently raise it through the course of the test and the subsequent Mixed papers.

- Mixed papers are longer tests containing a full range of maths question types. These are designed to provide rigorous practice with less challenging questions, perhaps against the clock, in order to help children acquire and develop the necessary skills and techniques for 11+ success.

Full answers are provided for both types of test in the middle of the book.

Some questions may require a ruler or protractor. Calculators are not permitted.

How much time should the tests take?

The tests are for practice and to reinforce learning, and you may wish to test exam techniques by working to a set time limit. Using the Mixed papers, we would recommend that your child spends 50 minutes answering the 50 questions in each paper.

You can reduce the suggested time by 5 minutes to practise working at speed.

Using the Progress Chart

The Progress Chart can be used to track Focus test and Mixed paper results over time to monitor how well your child is doing and identify any repeated problems in tackling the different question types.

Focus test 1 — Place value

1. Read this and write it as a number.

   | one hundred and fifty-eight thousand two hundred and four |

   _____

2. Write the number that is 1000 more than 282 450. _____

3. Use these four digits and the decimal point to make the largest possible decimal number between 20 and 30.

   Decimal numbers are whole numbers divided into tenths, hundredths and thousandths. A decimal point is used to separate whole numbers from decimals.

   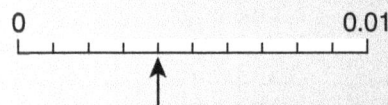

   This shows thousandths.

   0.004 is the same as $\dfrac{4}{1000}$

   ___ ___ . ___ ___

4. I'm thinking of a number less than 1. The two digits total 9 and it rounds to 0.2 to the nearest tenth.

   What number is it? 0 . ___ ___

5. Write the missing numbers in these. Choose from **10**, **100** or **1000**.

   28.09 × _____ = 2809

   73.65 ÷ _____ = 7.365

   0.072 × _____ = 72

6. Change this length from metres into centimetres and millimetres.

Metres	Centimetres	Millimetres
9.35 m	_____ cm	_____ mm

7 These are the heights of four boys. Write them in order, starting with the tallest.

> If you need to put decimals in order, write them out one under the other, lining up the decimal points.

Ali   1.22 m

Ben   1.29 m

Chen   1.18 m

David   1.2 m

_____ m   _____ m   _____ m   _____ m

8 Circle the smallest number and underline the largest number.

34.9   3.092   3.9   3.903   34.87   34.295

9 Write these in order.

9.405   9.045   9.45

_____ < _____ < _____

To round to the nearest tenth, look at the hundredths digit.

- If it is 5 or more, round up to the next tenth.
- If it is less than 5, the tenth digit stays the same.

Examples

4.86 rounds up to 4.9

2.614 rounds down to 2.6

---

10 Round each amount to the nearest tenth.

3.855 rounds to _____

17.806 rounds to _____

11 What is £46.38 to the nearest 10p? £_____

12 Round 235.48 m to the nearest whole metre. _____

Now go to the Progress Chart to record your score!   Total ◯ 12

Focus test 2 — Multiplication and division

Answer these. Show your method.

1) 56
   × 9
   ‾‾‾

2) 24
   × 8
   ‾‾‾

3) 45
   × 7
   ‾‾‾

4 Circle the multiplication with the largest product.

56 × 43   53 × 64   46 × 54

With the grid method for multiplication, multiply each pair of numbers to complete the grid. Then add up each row to find the total.

What is 37 multiplied by 43?

×	30	7
40	1200	280	→ 1480
3	90	21	→ + 111

Total = 1591

---

5 Use this grid to multiply 58 by 26.

×	50	8
20			→ _____
6			→ + _____

Total = _____

6 Use this grid to help you multiply 358 by 30.

×	300	50	8		
30				→	= ______

Before working out a division, think about an approximate answer first.

Example: What is 659 divided by 4?

```
   164 r3
4)659
 -400     (4 × 100)
  259
 -240     (4 × 60)
   19
 - 16     (4 × 4)     659 ÷ 4 = 164 remainder 3
    3
```

$$4\overline{)6^{2}5^{1}9}\quad 164 \text{ r}3$$

Complete these calculations.

7 $3\overline{)678}$

8 $5\overline{)297}$ r ___

9 $4\overline{)985}$ r ___

10 Circle the division that has a remainder of 3.

194 ÷ 5 306 ÷ 9 976 ÷ 8 295 ÷ 4

11 At a party, 75 glasses are needed for drinks. There are 6 glasses in a pack.

How many packs are needed so that there are enough glasses? ______

12 Beads are put on necklaces in sets of 9. How many complete necklaces can be made from 176 beads? ______

Now go to the Progress Chart to record your score! Total ◯ 12

Focus test 3 — Factors, multiples and prime numbers

> Factors are those numbers that will divide exactly into other numbers. Factors of numbers can be put into pairs:
>
> Factors of 21 → (1, 21) (3, 7)   21 has four factors.
>
> Factors of 28 → (1, 28) (2, 14) (4, 7) 28 has six factors.
>
> 7 is a *common factor* of 21 and 28.

1 Cross out the numbers that are **not** factors of 24.

   1   2   3   4   5   6   7   8   9   10   11   12

2 Write the missing factors of 60.

   60 → (1, 60) (2, __) (3, __) (__, __) (__, __) (__, __)

3 Write the factors of 72 in order, starting with the smallest.

   _____

4 What are the **common factors** of 18 and 42?

   1, __, __ and __

> A prime number only has two factors, 1 and itself. For example, 13 is a prime number as it can only be divided exactly by 1 and 13.

5 What is the next prime number after 20? ____

6 Complete these sentences with **always**, **sometimes** or **never**.

   A prime number will _____ have an odd number of factors.

   A square number will _____ have an odd number of factors.

7 Which two consecutive **prime** numbers multiply to make 77?

___ × ___ = 77

> A multiple is a number made by multiplying together two other numbers. For example, the multiples of 3 are 3, 6, 9, 12, 15, and so on.
>
> 12 is a <u>common multiple</u> of 3 and 4 because 4 × 3 = 12

8 Circle the numbers that are multiples of both 6 and 5.

    45   60   15   30   50

9 Write each of these numbers in the correct place on the Venn diagram.

    35   60   42   56

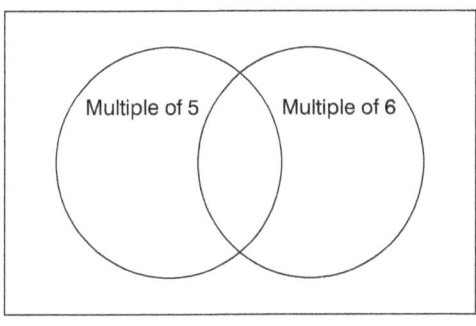

10 What is the smallest number that is a common multiple of 9 and 6? ___

11 Circle the square numbers in this set.

    81   36   18   56   100   48   64

12 The next square number after 144 is 169.

True or False? _____

Now go to the Progress Chart to record your score!   Total   12

Focus test 4 — Fractions, decimals, percentages, ratio and proportion

Equivalent fractions have the same value, even though they may look different.

$$\frac{6}{9} = \frac{2}{3}$$

To write $\frac{6}{9}$ in its lowest terms it is simplified to $\frac{2}{3}$.

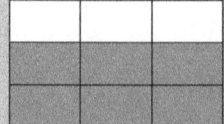

Write the fraction of each shape that is shaded. Express each fraction in its lowest terms.

1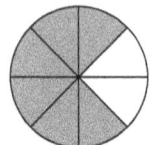

2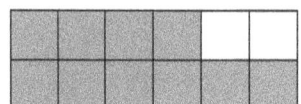

3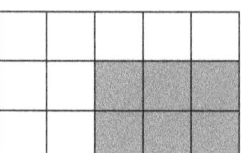

_____   _____   _____

Answer the questions about this rectangle.

4 What fraction of this rectangle is shaded? Write the fraction in its lowest terms. _____

5 Circle the percentage that is shaded.

12%   20%   60%
    30%   15%

6 Shade more of the squares so that 75% is shaded in total.

7 Six pens cost a total of £2.40. What is the cost of ten of these pens?

£_____

To change fractions to percentages, make them out of 100. This means you need to find the equivalent fraction with the denominator 100.

Example

$\frac{2}{5}$ is equivalent to $\frac{40}{100}$ = 40%

To change a percentage to a fraction, make it a fraction out of 100 and then simplify it.

Example

20% is $\frac{20}{100}$ which is the same as $\frac{1}{5}$

8 Convert each of these fractions to decimals and percentages.

Fraction	$\frac{3}{5}$	$\frac{9}{100}$	$\frac{7}{20}$	$\frac{4}{25}$	$\frac{1}{2}$
Decimal					
Percentage					

9 Put the fractions from this chart in order of size, starting with the smallest value.

_____   _____   _____   _____   _____

10 Circle the smallest decimal and underline the largest decimal.

0.04   0.15   0.32   0.1   0.06   0.27

Ratio is used to compare one amount with another.

Example

What is the ratio of white to black squares?

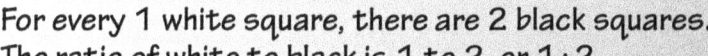

For every 1 white square, there are 2 black squares. The ratio of white to black is 1 to 2, or 1 : 2.

The proportion of squares that are white is 1 in every 3, or $\frac{1}{3}$

If this pattern was continued so there were 30 squares altogether, 10 would be white and 20 would be black.

11 A box of chocolates is filled with milk chocolates and plain chocolates in the ratio of 1 : 3. Complete the chart and then answer the questions.

Milk chocolates	1	2	3	4	5	6
Plain chocolates	3	6				
Total	4					

What proportion of the chocolates are milk chocolate? _____

How many plain chocolates are there in a box of 40 chocolates? _____

12 Sam mixes 1 litre of white paint with every 4 litres of blue paint. He needs 15 litres of paint altogether. How many litres of blue paint will he need? _____ litres

Now go to the Progress Chart to record your score!   Total ◯ 12

Focus test 5 Sequences

> A sequence is a list of numbers in a pattern. You can often find the rule for a sequence by looking at the difference between the numbers.
>
> What is the next number in this sequence?
>
> 58 49 40 31 22 __
>
> Each number is 9 less than the previous one, so the next number is 13. The rule is 'subtract 9'.

1 Write the next number in each sequence.

   14.5   15   15.5   16   ____

   $\frac{1}{4}$ $\frac{1}{2}$ $\frac{3}{4}$ 1   ____

   37   31   25   19   ____

2 Write the missing number in each sequence.

   19   69   ____   169   219

   8.7   7.8   ____   6   5.1

3 Write the rule for this sequence.

   −13   −8   −3   2   7   12

   The rule is _____

4 Will 50 be in this sequence? Yes or No? ____

5 Continue this pattern.

1   4   9   16   25   36   ___   ___

6 What is the name for these numbers? _____

7 Write the next two numbers in this sequence.

−9   −20   −31   −42   ___   ___

8 Write the next number in each sequence.

$\frac{1}{3}$ $\frac{2}{3}$ 1 $1\frac{1}{3}$ ___

$3\frac{3}{4}$ $4\frac{1}{4}$ $4\frac{3}{4}$ $5\frac{1}{4}$ ___

9 Write the missing numbers in this sequence.

___   14   34   54   74   ___

10 Write the rule for this sequence.

17   9   1   −7   −15

The rule is _____

11 Write the next two numbers in this sequence.

0.75   0.66   0.57   0.48   ___   ___

12 What are the next three numbers in this sequence?

1   1   2   3   5   8   ___   ___   ___

Focus test 6 — Equations and algebra

Equations have letters or symbols instead of numbers in a calculation.

$2n = 12$

$\triangle - 3 = 8$

$\square + 4 = 10$

You use the numbers given to work out the value of the symbol or letter.

$2n$ means n multiplied by 2. The multiplication sign × isn't used in equations because it looks like a letter.

What number does each letter represent?

1. $12 - y = 8$ $\qquad y = $ ___

2. $5c = 15$ $\qquad c = $ ___

3. $\dfrac{21}{x} = 3$ $\qquad x = $ ___

Write the value of each letter in these equations.

4. $3c + 1 = 7$ $\qquad c = $ ___

5. $4n - 5 = 7$ $\qquad n = $ ___

6. $\dfrac{a}{2} - 3 = 1$ $\qquad a = $ ___

Answer these, for the following values:

$a = 4 \qquad b = 3 \qquad c = 5$

7. $3a + 5 = $ _____

8. $4b + 2c = $ _____

9. $5a + b + 3c = $ _____

> A formula uses letters or words to give a rule.
> (The plural of formula is formulae.)

P = perimeter

S = sides

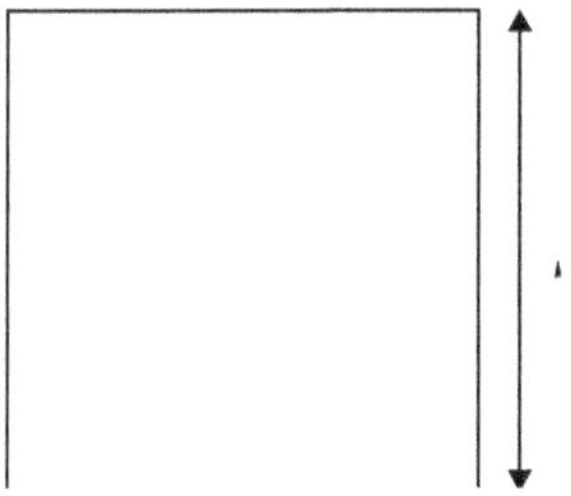

We use the formula $P = 4S$ to find the perimeter of a square.

10 What is the perimeter of a square with sides of 3.5 cm? _____ cm

This table records the number of pencils in boxes.

Boxes	1	2	3	4	5	n
Number of pencils	4	8	___	___	___	___

11 Write the missing number of pencils on the chart.

Look at the chart and write a formula for the total number of pencils in each box. _____

12 How many pencils will there be in 50 boxes? _____

Now go to the Progress Chart to record your score!   Total   12

Focus test 7 — Shapes and angles

Here are the properties of different quadrilaterals:

Square	Rectangle	Rhombus
4 equal sides 4 equal angles	 2 pairs of equal sides 4 right angles	 4 equal sides opposite sides parallel opposite angles equal
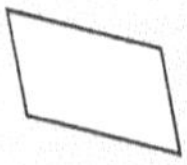 **Parallelogram** opposite sides equal and parallel opposite angles equal	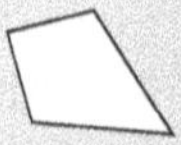 **Kite** 2 pairs of adjacent sides equal	 **Trapezium** 1 pair of parallel sides

1 Name these quadrilaterals.

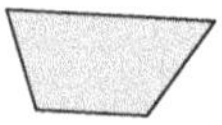

_____   _____   _____

Is each statement true or false? Circle the answer.

2 A trapezium always has a pair of parallel sides.   True / False

3 A kite is always symmetrical.   True / False

4 A rhombus always has pairs of opposite angles the same size.

True / False

5 How many lines of symmetry are there on a regular octagon? _____

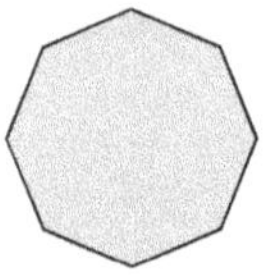

The net of a shape is what it looks like when it is opened out flat.

Example Net of a cuboid

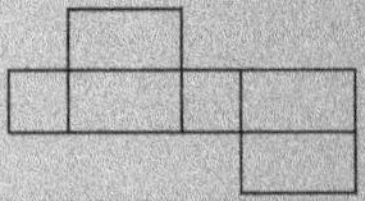

6 What shape is made from this net? 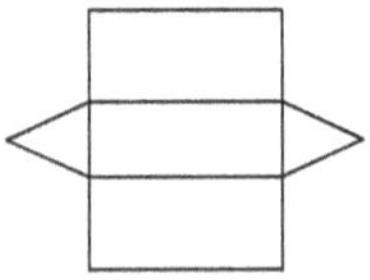   **7** Draw a net of a cube on this grid.

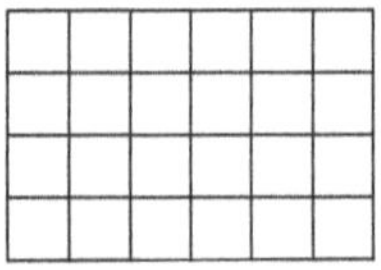

_____

_____

8 Complete this chart.

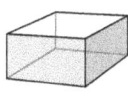

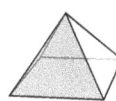

Name of shape	Number of faces	Number of vertices	Number of edges
Cuboid	____	____	____
Square-based pyramid	____	____	____

9 Write the names of these shapes.

____

____

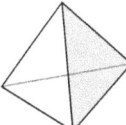

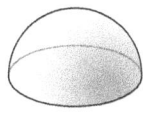

10 Calculate the size of angle *a* in this triangle.

Do not use a protractor.

Angle a = __°

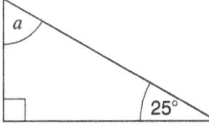

11 What is the size of the missing angle?

Do not use a protractor.

Angle x = __°

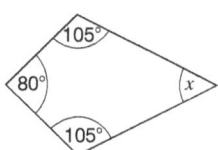

All the angles of a triangle add up to 180°.

$a + b + c = 180°$

All the angles of a quadrilateral add up to 360°.

$a + b + c + d = 360°$

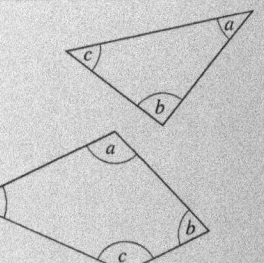

12 Measure these angles accurately with a protractor.

Angle a = _____° Angle b = _____°

Angle c = _____° Angle d = _____°

Now go to the Progress Chart to record your score! Total ___ 12

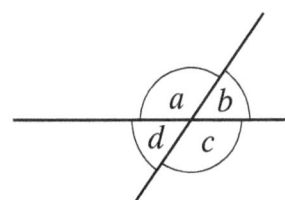

Focus test 8 — Area and perimeter

Area is usually measured in square centimetres or square metres, written as cm² and m². Always remember to write this at the end of the measurement.

The area of a rectangle is length × width.

Example

Area = 3 cm × 6 cm = 18 cm²

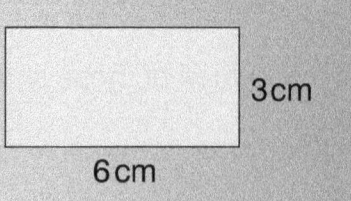

1. A rectangle has an area of 56 cm². One side is 8 cm long.

   What is the length of the side marked n?

   _____ cm

   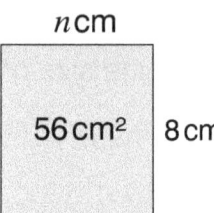

2. Draw a line between each pair of shapes with the same area.

   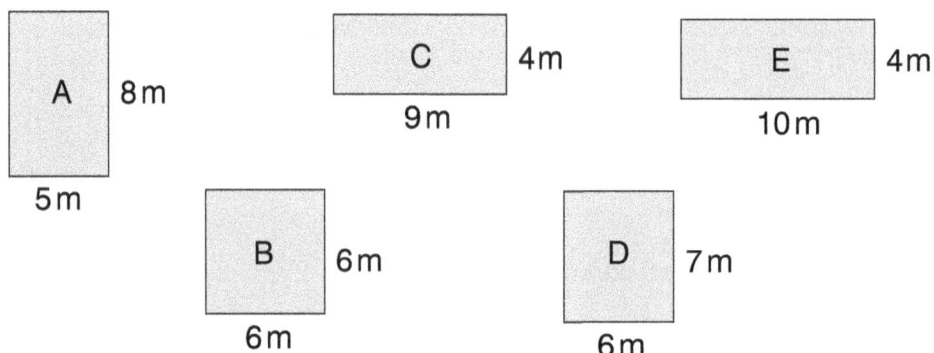

3. Calculate the area of this shape. _____ m²

   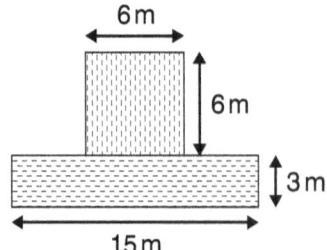

You can work out the perimeter of a rectangle by totalling the length and width and then doubling the total. Here is a formula for this:

2(length + width) or 2(*l* + w)

Perimeter = 2(6 + 4) = 20 cm

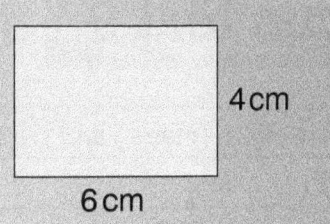

4 Draw a line between each pair of shapes with the same length perimeter.

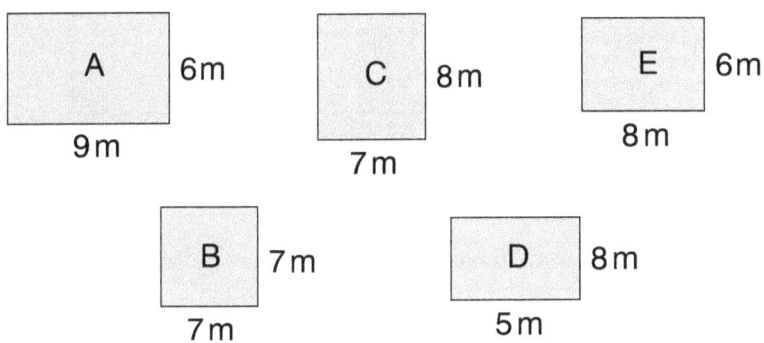

What is the area and perimeter of each of these rectangles?

5 Area = _____ cm²

6 Perimeter = _____ cm

9.5 cm
6 cm

7 Area = _____ cm²

8 Perimeter = _____ cm

35 cm
12 cm

9 A square has an area of 16 cm² and a perimeter of 16 cm.

What is the length of one side of this square? _____ cm

10 What is the area of a rectangular field that is 45 m by 100 m? _____ m²

What is the area and perimeter of this square?

11 Area = _____ cm²

12 Perimeter = _____ cm

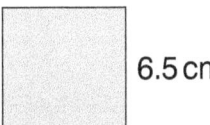

6.5 cm

Now go to the Progress Chart to record your score!   Total   12

Focus test 9 — Measures

> Length, weight (mass) and capacity are all measured using different units.
>
> **Length**
> 1 m (metre) = 100 cm (centimetres)   1 cm = 10 mm
>   = 1000 mm (millimetres)   1 km (kilometre) = 1000 m
>
> | Weight | Capacity |
> |---|---|
> | 1 kg (kilogram) = 1000 g (grams) | 1 l (litre) = 1000 ml (millilitres) |
> | 1 tonne = 1000 kg | 1 cl (centilitre) = 10 ml |
>
> Convert between units by multiplying or dividing by 10, 100 or 1000.
>
> **Examples**
> 1350 mm = 1.35 m   0.65 kg = 650 g   680 ml = 68 cl

1 Convert each of these lengths to complete the table.

Metres	Centimetres	Millimetres
0.95 m	_____ cm	_____ mm
_____ m	1240 cm	_____ mm
_____ m	_____ cm	6800 mm

2 How many millilitres are there in 8.5 l? _____ ml

3 How many kilograms are there in 4.7 tonnes? _____ kg

4 Which is heavier, 6.85 kg or 690 g? _____

5 Write these lengths in order, starting with the shortest.

   1.05 m   150 cm   105 mm   1550 cm

   _____   _____   _____   _____

   Shortest →

Imperial units are sometimes used. These are measures that were used in the past. Try to learn these approximate values.

Length	Weight	Capacity
2.5 cm ≈ 1 inch	28 g ≈ 1 ounce	1 litre ≈ 1.76 pints
30 cm ≈ 1 foot	1 kg ≈ 2.2 lb	4.5 litres ≈ 1 gallon
1 metre ≈ 3 feet		
8 km ≈ 5 miles		

Circle the best answer for each of these.

6 Approximately how many pints are there in 4 litres?

   3 pints   7 pints   10 pints   15 pints   18 pints

7 Approximately how many miles are there in 24 km?

   3 miles   10 miles   15 miles   20 miles   30 miles

8 What is the approximate length in centimetres of a tie 10 inches long?

   5 cm   14 cm   20 cm   25 cm   45 cm

9 What is the difference between the amount of water in these two jugs?

   _____ ml

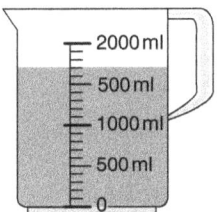 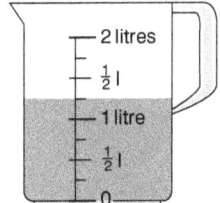

10 What is the total amount of water in these two jugs? _____ litres

11 A bus should arrive at 20:25 but it is 15 minutes late.

   What time will the bus actually arrive?

   Write the time on these two clocks.

    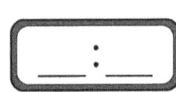

12 What is the difference in weight between these two parcels? Give your answer in grams.

   _____ g

   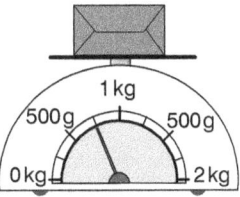 

Now go to the Progress Chart to record your score!   Total   12

Focus test 10: Coordinates and transformations

Coordinates are used to show positions on a grid.

Two numbers show the position. The number on the horizontal x-axis is written first, then the number on the vertical y-axis.

The coordinates of A are (−3, 4).

The coordinates of B are (−5, −2).

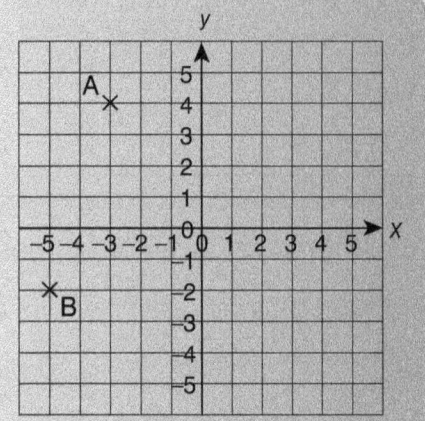

1 What are the coordinates of point A? (____ , ____)

2 What are the coordinates of point B? (____ , ____)

3 What are the coordinates of point C? (____ , ____)

4 A, B and C are three vertices of a rectangle. Plot the missing fourth vertex and label it D.

5 What are the coordinates of point D? (____ , ____)

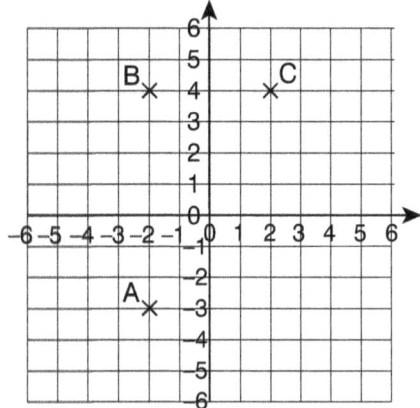

6 This is an isosceles triangle. What are the missing coordinates? Write them on the answer lines on the diagram.

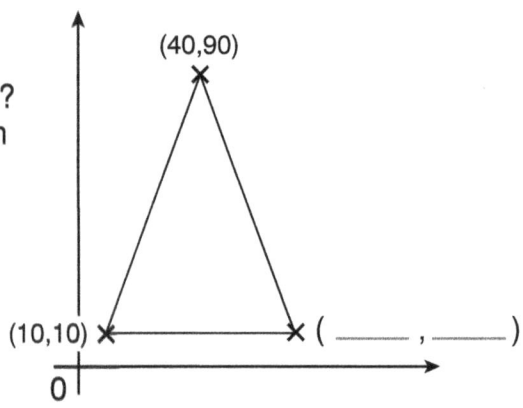

22

A shape can be moved in three ways.
- Rotation: the shape is rotated about a point, clockwise or anticlockwise.
- Reflection: this is sometimes called 'flipping over'.
- Translation: this is sliding a shape across, up, down or diagonally, without rotating or flipping over.

Write whether these shapes have been **translated**, **rotated** or **reflected**.

7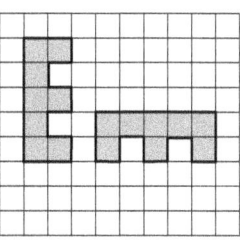

8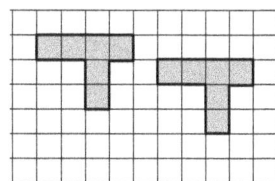

_____   _____

9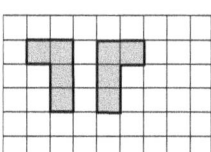

_____

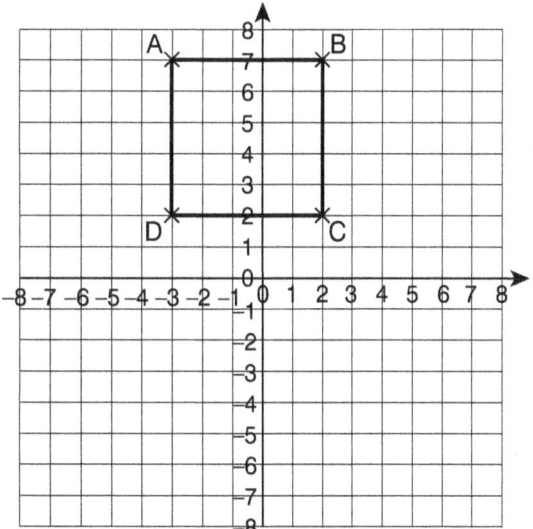

This square is translated. Point B moves to (6, 5) and point D moves to (1, 0).

10 Plot A_2, B_2, C_2 and D_2 on the grid and join the points to show the translated position of the square.

11–12 Where are points A_2 and C_2 on the translated shape?

A_2 (_____ , _____)

C_2 (_____ , _____)

Now go to the Progress Chart to record your score! Total ◯ 12

Focus test 11 — Charts, graphs and tables

This Venn diagram sorts the 26 letters of the alphabet.

Alphabet sort

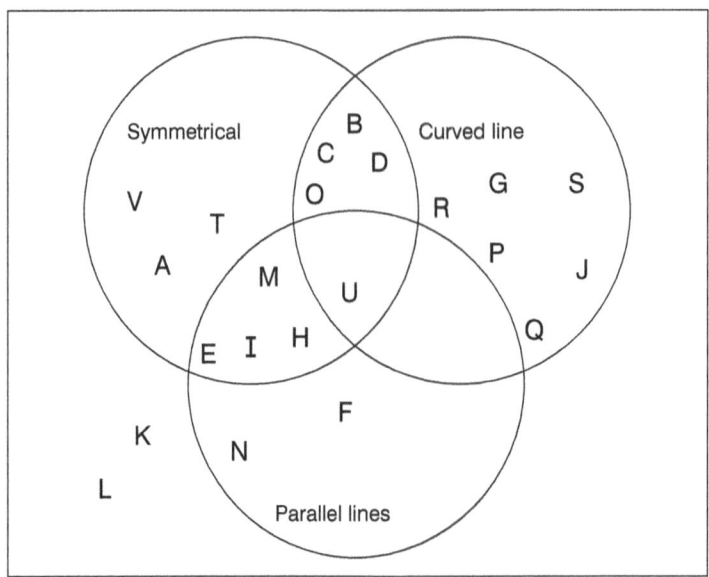

1. Write each of the last four letters of the alphabet in the correct place on the diagram.

    W   X   Y   Z

Look at the Venn diagram and answer these.

2. How many letters have one or more **curved lines** and are also **symmetrical**? _____

3. How many letters are **not** symmetrical? _____

4. How many letters have both **curved** and **parallel lines** but are **not symmetrical**? _____

5. Which letter is **symmetrical** and has both **curved** and **parallel** lines?
   _____

6. Which letters are **not symmetrical** and do **not** have **curved** or **parallel** lines? _____

To understand bar charts and other types of graphs, look carefully at the different parts of the graph before you look at the bars.
- Read the title. What is it about?
- Look at the axis labels. These give information about each axis.
- Work out the scale. Do the axes go up in 1s, 2s, 5s, 10s…?

The information from the Venn diagram has been drawn on a block graph.

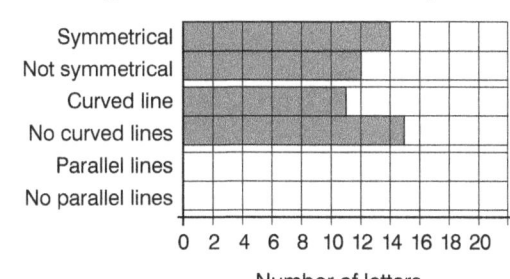

Sorting the 26 letters of the alphabet

7 Count the total number of letters with parallel lines and draw the missing block 'Parallel lines' on this graph. Remember, some will also have symmetrical and curved lines. Then, draw the missing block for 'No parallel lines'.

Use the information on the block graph to answer these.

8 How many letters are symmetrical? _____

9 How many letters have curved lines? _____

Pie charts are circles divided into sections. Each section shows a number of items so that they can be compared. You could be asked to give a fraction, a percentage or a number as an answer.

A bookshelf had 40 books on it. This pie chart shows the three types of books.

10 What fraction of the books are non-fiction? _____

11 What percentage of the books are fiction? _____%

12 How many of the books are poetry books? _____

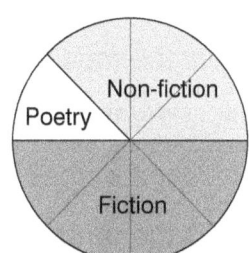

Focus test 12 — Mean, median, mode, range and probability

- The <u>mode</u> of a set of data is the item that occurs the most often.
- The <u>median</u> is the middle number in a set of numbers when arranged in order.
- The <u>mean</u> of a set of numbers is their total divided by the number of items.
- The <u>range</u> tells us how much the information is spread. To find the range, take the smallest value from the largest value.

These are the number of goals scored by a football team over 9 matches.

5   2   2   1   2   2   4   3   6

The mode is 2 because 2 goals were scored in 4 matches.

The median is 2 because 2 is in the middle when you arrange them in order:

1   2   2   2   2   3   4   5   6

The mean is 3. A total of 27 goals have been scored. Divide this by the number of games to get the mean: $27 \div 9 = 3$

The range is 5. This is the difference between the largest and smallest value: $6 - 1 = 5$

These are the lengths of seven worms measured in a science lesson.

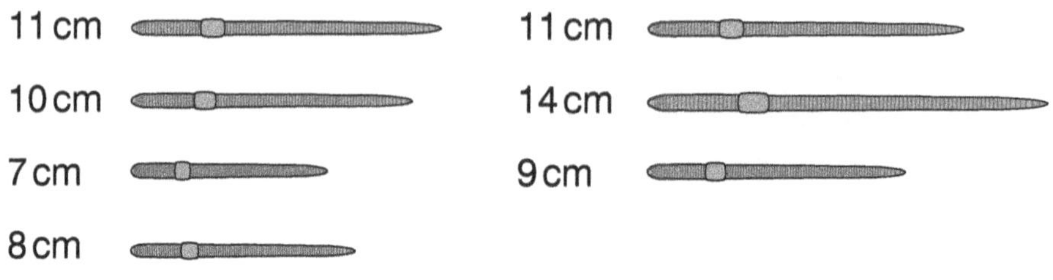

- 11 cm
- 10 cm
- 7 cm
- 8 cm
- 11 cm
- 14 cm
- 9 cm

1. What is the mean length of these worms? _____
2. What is the median length of these worms? _____
3. What is the mode? _____
4. What is the range? _____

Another two worms are measured and added to this group.

5 cm   6 cm

5 What is the mean length of all nine worms? _____

6 What is the median length of all nine worms? _____

7 What is the new mode? _____   **8** What is the new range? _____

'Even chance' means there is an equal chance of something happening or not happening. We also say a 1 in 2 or $\frac{1}{2}$ chance, or a 50:50 chance.

Examples

What is the probability of rolling an odd number on a fair dice?

There are 3 out of 6 numbers that are odd (1, 3 and 5). This means there is a 1 in 2 or $\frac{1}{2}$ chance that it will land on an odd number.

What is the probability of rolling a multiple of 3 on a dice?

There are 2 out of 6 numbers that are multiples of 3 (3 and 6). This means there is a 1 in 3 or $\frac{1}{3}$ chance that it will land on a multiple of 3.

A probability scale can be used to show how likely an event is to happen.

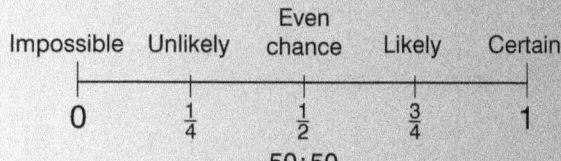

Write the likelihood of the spinner landing on each of these. Write each answer as a fraction in its lowest terms.

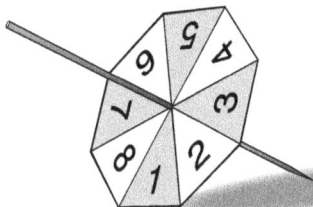

9 What is the likelihood of it landing on an even number? _____

10 What is the likelihood of it landing on a multiple of 3? _____

11 What is the likelihood of it landing on a number less than 7? _____

12 What is the likelihood of it landing on the number 1? _____

Mixed paper 1

Multiply each number by 1000.

1 8.2 _____ **2** 6.75 _____ **3** 91 _____

4 Write < or > to make this number sentence true. 0.518 ___ 0.581

5 What is the total weight of two boxes weighing 14.6 kg and 5.5 kg? _____

6 What is the difference between 483 km and 79 km? _____

Complete these calculations.

7 5)283 r ___   **8** 4)107 r ___   **9** 6)390

10 Multiply 16 by 9. _____

11–12 Write the missing factors of 45.

45 → (1, 45) (3, ___) (___, 9)

13–14 Which of these numbers are multiples of both 8 and 3? Circle them.

16   28   21   32   48   24   60

Change each maths test score to a percentage.

15 $\frac{45}{50}$ → ___%   **16** $\frac{32}{50}$ → ___%

Choose the correct decimal for each of these.

0.25   0.2   0.52   0.5

17 50% = ___   **18** $\frac{1}{4}$ = ___

Write the next number in each sequence.

19 4   2   0   −2   −4   ___

20 2.5   3   3.5   4   4.5   ___

21 767   667   567   467   367   _____

22 4   9   16   25   36   _____

Jamie built piles of bricks. Each new pile was a row taller than the pile before.

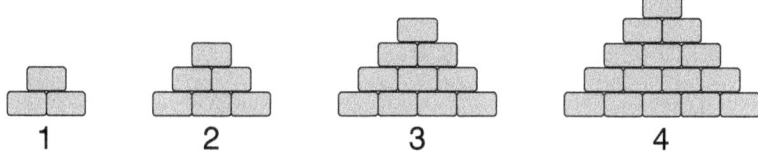

1   2   3   4

23–25 This table records the number of bricks in each pile. Write the missing numbers.

Pile	1	2	3	4	n
Number of bricks	3	___	___	___	?

26 How many bricks will there be in the next pile of bricks in this pattern? _____

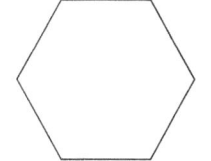

27 What is the name of this shape? _____

28 How many lines of symmetry are there on this shape? ____

29 All the angles are the same size in this shape. Circle the word that describes these angles.

    reflex   acute   right   obtuse

30 How many pairs of parallel sides are there on this shape? ____

31 Draw a line to join the two shapes with the same size area.

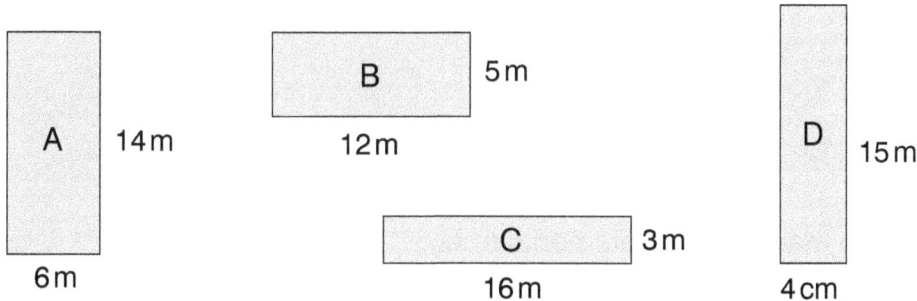

32 Tick the two shapes with the same length perimeter.

33 A rectangle has an area of 63 cm². One side is 7 cm long. What is the length of the side marked x? _____ cm

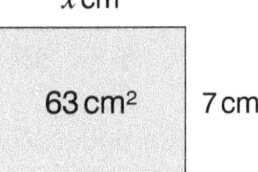

34 Calculate the area of this whole shape. _____ m²

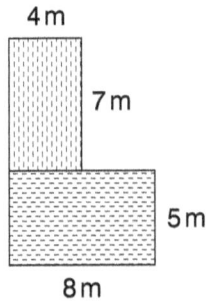

35 What is the length of this line in millimetres? _____ mm

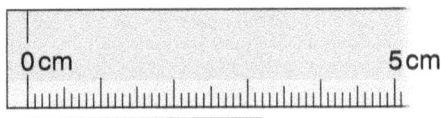

36 What is the weight of this parcel? _____ kg

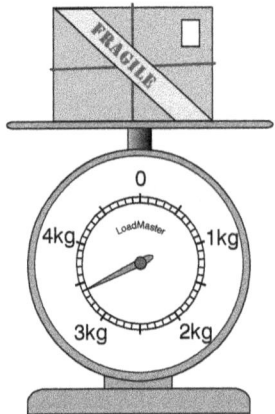

Write <, > or = to make these statements true.

37 1700 ml ___ 1.7 litres

38 4.5 kg ___ 450 g

Explanations in the main text of the book are referred to *by their page*; all other questions referred to can be found in the answer section.

Any answer that requires units of measurement should be marked wrong if the correct units have not been included.

Focus test 1 (pages 4–5)

1 **158 204** Insert the number into a place value grid to help write the answer.

HTh	TTh	Th	H	T	O
1	5	8	2	0	4

2 **283 450** The second 2 is in the thousands place, so increase this digit by 1.
3 **28.61** As the number is between 20 and 30, the first digit must be 2; write the rest of the numbers from largest to smallest.
4 **0.18** If the digit to the right of the one being rounded to is 5 or more, the digit being rounded to increases by 1; if the digit to the right is 4 or less, it remains the same (e.g. 0.17 becomes 0.2 and 0.14 becomes 0.1 when rounded to the nearest tenth). As the number rounds to 0.2, it must be between 0.15 and 0.24; of these possible answers, only 0.18 has 2 digits that add up to 9.
5 **100, 10, 1000** When multiplying or dividing a number by 10, 100 or 1000, it is moved across the decimal point. It moves to the left if it has been multiplied and to the right if divided. When multiplied or divided by 10 it moves 1 place, by 100 it moves 2 places, by 1000 it moves 3 places. Insert the numbers on the grid and count how many spaces they are moved to find the answers.

Th	H	T	O	.	t	h	th	
		2	8	.	0	9		
2	8	0	9	.				28.09 × 100 = 2809
		7	3	.	6	5		
			7	.	3	6	5	73.65 ÷ 10 = 7.365
			0	.	0	7	2	
0	0	7	2	.				0.072 × 1000 = 72

6 **935 cm, 9350 mm** Refer to Q5 on multiplying by 100 and 10; 1 m = 100 cm so multiply by 100 (9.35 × 100 = 935) and 1 cm = 10 mm so multiply that answer by 10 (935 × 10 = 9350).

7 **1.29 m, 1.22 m, 1.2 m, 1.18 m** Insert the numbers into a grid ensuring the decimal points are lined up and add 0 in any gaps after the decimal point (1.2 is the same as 1.20). The largest number will be the tallest. To look for the largest number, find the largest digit in each column, starting on the left and, if any are the same, find the largest in the next column to the right.

1	.	2	2
1	.	2	9
1	.	1	8
1	.	2	0

8 **3.092**, **34.9** Refer to Q7 on ordering decimal numbers; to find the smallest number, look for the smallest digit in each column.
9 **9.045 < 9.405 < 9.45** < means less than so the first number will be the smallest; refer to Q7 on ordering decimal numbers and look for the smallest digit in each column.
10–12 Refer to Q4 on rounding.
10 **3.9, 17.8** In 3.855, 8 is in the tenths place and 5 is to its right, so 8 increases by 1; in 17.806, 8 is in the tenths place and 0 is to its right, so 8 remains the same.
11 **£46.40** 3 is in the tenths (10p) place and 8 is to its right, so 3 increases by 1; money is always written with 2 digits after the decimal, so change the digit in the hundredths (1p) place to 0.
12 **235 m** Round to the digit in the ones place to round to the nearest whole number; 5 is in the ones place and 4 is to its right, so it remains the same.

Focus test 2 (pages 6–7)

1–3 When using column multiplication, work from right to left and add on any numbers carried over as shown for Q1.

```
        5  6
    ×      9
    ───────
    5  0  4
       5  5
```

1 **504**
2 **192**
3 **315**

4 **53 × 64** The product is the answer when two numbers are multiplied together (e.g. the product of 4 and 2 is 8). Use long multiplication, as shown for the first equation (56 × 43). First, multiply 56 by the 3 in the ones column to find 168. Then place a zero in the ones place on the next row in the answer and multiply 56 by 4 to find 224. Finally, add the 2 answers together;
168 + 2240 = 2408

```
          5  6
     ×    4  3
     ─────────
          1  6  8
   +   2  2  4  0
     ─────────
       2  4  0  8
```

5 **1508** 20 × 50 = 1000 and 20 × 8 = 160;
6 × 50 = 300 and 6 × 8 = 48; 1000 + 160 = 1160 and 300 + 48 = 348; 1160 + 348 = 1508

×	50	8		
20	1000	160	→	1160
6	300	48	→	+ 348
			Total	= 1508

6 **10 740** 30 × 300 = 9000, 30 × 50 = 1500 and 30 × 8 = 240; 9000 + 1500 + 240 = 10 740

×	300	50	8		
30	9000	1500	240	→	= 10740

7–12 Choose the method that is easier to complete the equation with. An example of using long division (the method shown is also called 'chunking') and short division is shown in Q7. Think about the approximation of your answer, too.

7 **226** An approximation of this calculation would be something a little more than 200 because 200 × 3 = 600. 'Chunking' is where lots of 100s and 10s are subtracted to help find the answer; 3 lots of 200 = 600, so subtract this from 678 to find 78; 3 lots of 20 are 60, so subtract this from 78 to find 18; 3 lots of 6 are 18, so subtract 18 to find a remainder of 0; finally, add together the lots of 3 that have been subtracted to find the answer (200 + 20 + 6 = 226).

```
              2   2   6
       ┌───────────────
    3  │  6   7   8
    -     6   0   0      (3 × 200)
       ───────────
              7   8
    -         6   0      (3 × 20)
           ───────────
                  1   8
    -             1   8  (3 × 6)
              ───────────
                      0
```

Using short division, 3 goes into 6 twice so write 2 above the 6; 3 goes into 7 two times and there is a remainder of 1, so write 2 above the 7 and 1 in front of 8 to form the number 18; 3 goes into 18 six times so write 6 above it.

```
          2   2   6
       ┌───────────
    3  │  6   7  ¹8
```

8 **59 r 2** An approximation of this calculation would be 60 because 60 × 5 = 300.
9 **246 r 1** An approximation of this calculation would be 250 because 250 × 4 = 1000.
10 **295 ÷ 4** 295 ÷ 4 = 73 r 3
11 **13** 75 ÷ 6 = 12 r 3; 12 packs will only contain 72 so 13 packs will be needed.
12 **19** 176 ÷ 9 = 19 r 5 so only 19 can be made.

Focus test 3 (pages 8–9)

1–4 Refer to the explanation of factors on page 8.
1 **not factors of 24: 5, 7, 9, 10, 11** (1 × 24), (2 × 12), (3 × 8) and (4 × 6) all equal 24.
2 **(1, 60) (2, 30) (3, 20) (4, 15) (5, 12) (6, 10)**
3 **1, 2, 3, 4, 6, 8, 9, 12, 18, 24, 36, 72** (1 × 72), (2 × 36), (3 × 24), (4 × 18), (6 × 12) and (8 × 9) all equal 72.
4 **1, 2, 3 and 6** Write the factors of 18 and 42 and find numbers that appear in both groups; factors of 18 are **1, 2, 3, 6**, 9, 18 and factors of 42 are **1, 2, 3, 6**, 7, 14, 21, 42.
5 **23** 21 and 22 have too many factors; 23 is the next number that has only 2 factors (1 and 23).
6 **never, always** A prime number only has 2 factors, so will never have an odd number; a square number is the answer when a number is multiplied by itself (e.g. 5 × 5 = 25) and this number only needs to be written once (e.g. factors of 25 are 1, 5 and 25), so it will always have an odd number.
7 **7 × 11** Consecutive numbers are numbers that appear next to each other in a list; the first six prime numbers are: 2, 3, 5, 7, 11, 13; use times tables knowledge to find the answer; 77 is in the 7 and 11 times table and 7 × 11 = 77.

8 **30, 60** 5 × 6 = 30; 12 × 5 = **60** and 10 × 6 = **60**

9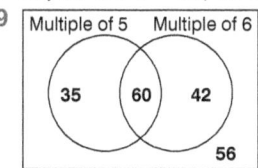

As 60 is a multiple of 5 and 6 it is placed in the section where the circles overlap; 35 is only a multiple of 5 so it is placed in the remainder of the left circle and 42 is only a multiple of 6 so it is placed in the remainder of the right circle. As 56 is not a multiple of 5 or 6 it is placed outside both circles.

10 **18** The answer will not be higher than 54 as 9 × 6 = 54; write the multiples of both numbers up to 54 and find the lowest number that is in both groups.

11–12 Refer to Q6 on square numbers.

11 **81, 36, 100, 64** 9 × 9 = **81**; 6 × 6 = **36**; 10 × 10 = **100**; 8 × 8 = **64**

12 **True** 12 × 12 = 144 so the next one will be the answer to 13 × 13; partition 13 to multiply; 10 × 13 = 130 and 3 × 13 = 39; 130 + 39 = 169

Focus test 4 (pages 10–11)

1–4 To find the fraction shown on a shape, count the shaded sections to find the numerator (top number) and count all the sections to find the denominator (bottom number). To change a fraction into its 'lowest terms' (also called simplifying), divide the numerator and denominator by the same number.

1 $\frac{3}{4}$ 6 out of 8 sections have been shaded so $\frac{6}{8}$ is shown; 6 and 8 can both be divided by 2 (6 ÷ 2 = 3 and 8 ÷ 2 = 4) so $\frac{6}{8} = \frac{3}{4}$.

2 $\frac{5}{6}$ 10 out of 12 sections have been shaded so $\frac{10}{12}$ is shown; 10 and 12 can both be divided by 2 (10 ÷ 2 = 5 and 12 ÷ 2 = 6) so $\frac{10}{12} = \frac{5}{6}$.

3 $\frac{2}{5}$ 6 out of 15 sections have been shaded so $\frac{6}{15}$ is shown; 6 and 15 can both be divided by 3 (6 ÷ 3 = 2 and 15 ÷ 3 = 5) so $\frac{6}{15} = \frac{2}{5}$.

4 $\frac{3}{5}$ 12 out of 20 sections have been shaded so $\frac{12}{20}$ is shown; 12 and 20 can both be divided by 4 (12 ÷ 4 = 3 and 20 ÷ 4 = 5) so $\frac{12}{20} = \frac{3}{5}$.

5 **60%** Refer to the explanation of changing fractions into percentages on page 10 and make sure both digits in the fraction are multiplied by the same number; $\frac{12}{20} = \frac{60}{100}$ (as 12 × 5 = 60 and 20 × 5 = 100); the numerator shown is the same as the percentage; $\frac{60}{100} = 60\%$

6 **Check another three squares have been shaded.** Refer to the explanation of changing percentages into fractions on page 10; 75% = $\frac{75}{100}$ which can be simplified to $\frac{15}{20}$ so 15 out of 20 squares need to shaded.

7 **£4 (or £4.00)** £1.00 = 100p, so £2.40 = 240p; divide by 6 to find the cost of 1 pen (240p ÷ 6 = 40p) then multiply to find the cost of 10 (40p × 10 = 400p); 400p = £4.00

8

Fraction	$\frac{3}{5}$	$\frac{9}{100}$	$\frac{7}{20}$	$\frac{4}{25}$	$\frac{1}{2}$
Decimal	0.6	0.09	0.35	0.16	0.5
Percentage	60%	9%	35%	16%	50%

Find the equivalent of each fraction with a denominator of 100 by multiplying both digits by the same number (for example, $\frac{3}{5} = \frac{60}{100}$ as 3 × 20 = 60 and 5 × 20 = 100). The numerator can then be written as the 2 digits after the decimal point and as a percentage (e.g. $\frac{60}{100}$ = 0.60 and 60%). If the numerator only has 1 digit, insert another 0 after the decimal point (e.g. $\frac{9}{100}$ = 0.09). Remember 0.60 is the same as 0.6 and so on.

9 $\frac{9}{100}, \frac{4}{25}, \frac{7}{20}, \frac{1}{2}, \frac{3}{5}$ Put the percentages in order (9%, 16%, 35%, 50%, 60%) then write their equivalent fractions in the same order.

10 **0.4**, **0.32** Refer to Focus test 1 Q7 on ordering decimal numbers; to find the smallest number, look for the smallest digit in each column.

11 $\frac{1}{4}$, **30**

Milk chocolates	1	2	3	4	5	6
Plain chocolates	3	6	9	12	15	18
Total	4	8	12	16	20	24

For every 1 milk chocolate there are 3 plain ones, so multiply the number of milk chocolates by 3 each time and add the numbers in each column to find the total; 1 in every 4 is milk chocolate so it is $\frac{1}{4}$; in the first column, it shows 3 in every 4 are plain chocolates, so multiply both numbers by 10 to find 30 in every 40 will be plain.

12 **12 litres** 1 litre + 4 litres = 5 litres; 5 litres × 3 = 15 litres, so multiply by 3; 3 × 4 litres of blue paint = 12.

Focus test 5 (pages 12–13)

1–3 In a sequence, if the numbers increase in size, they have been added to or multiplied; if they decrease, they have been subtracted from or divided. Check for addition or subtraction first by finding the difference between numbers next to one another. If this does not work, then try multiplying or dividing.

1. **16.5, $1\frac{1}{4}$, 13** 15 is the same as 15.0 and 15.0 − 14.5 = 0.5; the numbers increase so the rule is 'add 0.5'; to subtract decimal numbers, line up the decimal points and subtract in the same way as whole numbers; remember to borrow if the digit at the top is smaller than the one below it, for example:

   ```
     1  ⁴5 . ¹0
   − 1   4 .  5
   ─────────────
     0   0 .  5
   ```

   16 + 0.5 = **16.5**. $\frac{1}{2}$ is the equivalent of $\frac{2}{4}$ and $\frac{2}{4} + \frac{1}{4} = \frac{3}{4}$ so the rule is 'add $\frac{1}{4}$'; $1 + \frac{1}{4} = 1\frac{1}{4}$. 37 − 31 = 6 and the numbers decrease so the rule is 'subtract 6'; 19 − 6 = 13

2. **119, 6.9** 69 − 19 = 50; the numbers increase, so the rule is 'add 50'; 69 + 50 = 119; 8.7 − 7.8 = 0.9; the numbers decrease, so the rule is 'subtract 0.9'; 7.8 − 0.9 = 6.9

3. **The rule is add 5.** Negative numbers 'mirror' whole numbers, as shown on the number line where the numbers increase in size from left to right. Find the difference between the whole numbers (7 − 2 = 5); the numbers increase so the rule is 'add 5'.

   −14 −13 −12 −11 −10 −9 −8 −7 −6 −5 −4 −3 −2 −1 0 1 2 3 4 5 6 7 8 9 10 11 12 13 14

4. **No** As 5 is being added, the digit in the ones place will alternate between 7 and 2 (17, 22, 27, 32, 37, 42 and so on); alternatively, continue adding 5 up to 50 (42 + 5 = 47; 47 + 5 = 52 so it cannot be in the sequence).

5. **49, 64** The numbers increase but not by the same interval so it cannot be addition. Use times tables knowledge: 1 × 1 = 1, 2 × 2 = 4, 3 × 3 = 9, and so on: 7 × 7 = 49 and 8 × 8 = 64.

6. **square numbers** A square number is the answer when a number has been multiplied by itself, e.g. 5 × 5 = 25.

7. **−53, −64** Refer to Q3 on negative numbers; the difference between −9 and −20 is 11 and the numbers decrease so the rule is 'subtract 11'; 11 subtracted from −42 = −53; 11 subtracted from −53 = −64.

8. **$1\frac{2}{3}, 5\frac{3}{4}$** $\frac{2}{3} - \frac{1}{3} = \frac{1}{3}$; the numbers increase so the rule is 'add $\frac{1}{3}$'; $1\frac{1}{3} + \frac{1}{3} = 1\frac{2}{3}$; write the fractions on a number line to find the difference between $3\frac{3}{4}$ and $4\frac{1}{4}$ is $\frac{2}{4}$: $5\frac{1}{4} + \frac{2}{4} = 5\frac{3}{4}$

   $3\frac{3}{4}$ 4 $4\frac{1}{4}$ $4\frac{2}{4}$ $4\frac{3}{4}$ 5 $5\frac{1}{4}$ $5\frac{2}{4}$ $5\frac{3}{4}$

9. **−6, 94** 34 − 14 = 20; the numbers increase so the rule is 'add 20'; −6 + 20 = 14 (refer to Q3 on negative numbers); 74 + 20 = 94

10. **The rule is subtract 8.** Refer to Q3 on negative numbers; 17 − 9 = 8; the numbers decrease so it is subtraction.

11. **0.39, 0.3** Refer to Q1 on subtracting decimal numbers; 0.75 − 0.66 = 0.09; the numbers decrease so the rule is 'subtract 0.09'; 0.48 − 0.09 = 0.39 and 0.39 − 0.09 = 0.30 (0.30 is the same as 0.3).

12. **13, 21, 34** 1 + 1 = 2; 1 + 2 = 3 and 2 + 3 = 5 so the numbers next to one another have been added together to find the next number; 5 + 8 = 13; 8 + 13 = 21; 13 + 21 = 34

Focus test 6 (pages 14–15)

1–6 Use the inverse to find the answers. The inverse of addition is subtraction and the inverse of multiplication is division. For example, 10 − ☐ = 3 can be inverted to 10 − 3 = ☐ or ☐ + 3 = 10 and 12 ÷ ☐ = 4 can be inverted to 12 ÷ 4 = ☐ or 4 × ☐ = 12.

1. **4** 12 − 8 = 4
2. **3** $5c = 5 \times c$; 15 ÷ 5 = 3
3. **7** $\frac{21}{x} = 21 \div x$; 21 ÷ 3 = 7
4. **2** 7 − 1 = 6 so 3c = 6 and 6 ÷ 3 = 2.
5. **3** 7 + 5 = 12 so 4n = 12 and 12 ÷ 4 = 3.
6. **8** $\frac{a}{2} = a \div 2$; 1 + 3 = 4 so $\frac{a}{2} = 4$ and 4 × 2 = 8
7. **17** 3 × 4 = 12 so 3a = 12; 12 + 5 = 17
8. **22** 4 × 3 = 12 so 4b = 12; 2 × 5 = 10 so 2c = 10; 12 + 10 = 22
9. **38** 5 × 4 = 20 so 5a = 20; b = 3; 3 × 5 = 15 so 3c = 15; 20 + 3 + 15 = 38
10. **14 cm** The perimeter of a shape is the total of all of its side lengths; all 4 sides on a square are equal in length. Use the formula
    p = 4s
    p = 4 × 3.5 cm
    p = 14 cm

11.
Boxes	1	2	3	4	5
Number of pencils	4	8	**12**	**16**	**20**

    p = 4n There are 4 pencils in each box, so multiply the number of boxes by 4 each time to find the number to insert below it. '*p*' can be used to represent each box (other letters are acceptable also) and, as there are 4 pencils in each box, this can be written as '4*n*' (with *n* representing each pencil) so 4*n* = *p* or *p* = 4*n*.

12. **200** Multiply the number of pencils in 1 box by 50; 4 × 50 = 200

Focus test 7 (pages 16–17)

1–4 Refer to the table on properties of quadrilaterals on page 16; rotate the page to look at the shapes from different angles.
1 **parallelogram, rhombus, trapezium**
2 **True** A pair of parallel lines are always the same distance apart from one another along their whole length. They never meet or cross.
3 **True** Lines of symmetry go through the middle of the shape, creating a 'mirror image' on each side of the line. As a kite has 2 pairs of sides that are equal length, there will always be a line of symmetry, as shown.

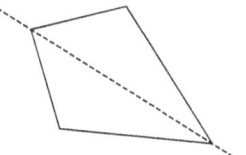

4 **True**
5 **8**

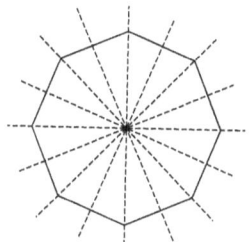

6 **triangular prism**

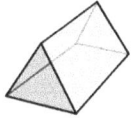

7 *This is one possible solution. Check the net will fold to make a cube.*

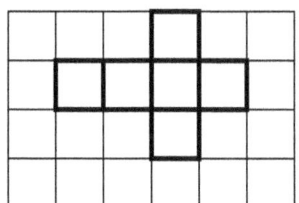

8

Name of shape	Number of faces	Number of vertices	Number of edges
Cuboid	6	8	12
Square-based pyramid	5	5	8

A face is a flat surface of a shape, an edge is where 2 faces meet and a vertex (plural = vertices) is a corner where 3 or more faces and edges meet.
9 **tetrahedron, hemisphere** A tetrahedron is also known as a triangular-based pyramid. Half of a sphere is shown, which is a hemisphere.
10–11 Refer to the explanations of angles in a triangle and a quadrilateral on page 17.
10 **65°** When an angle is shown as a small square, it is always 90°; 90° + 25° = 115°; 180° − 115° = 65°
11 **70°** 105° + 80° + 105° = 290°; 360° − 290° = 70°
12 **Angle a = 125°, Angle b = 55°, Angle c = 125°, Angle d = 55°** Make sure the line along the bottom of the protractor is laid over the line on the angle and the centre of the cross at the bottom of the protractor is placed over where the 2 lines meet. If the angle is larger than 90°, use the larger numbers on the protractor; if it is smaller, use the smaller numbers on the protractor. Opposite angles around a point are always the same size, so $a = c$ and $b = d$.

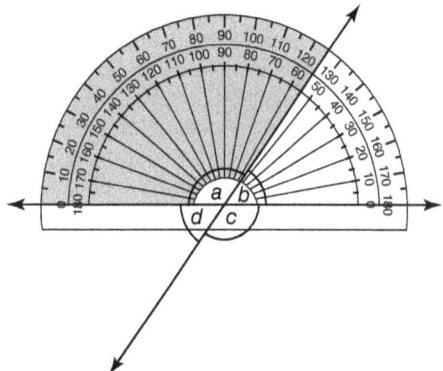

Focus test 8 (pages 18–19)

1 **7 cm** Use knowledge of times tables; 8 × 7 = 56
2 **A and E, B and C** Shape A = 40 cm² (5 × 8), shape B = 36 cm² (6 × 6), shape C = 36 cm² (9 × 4), shape D = 42 cm² (6 × 7) and shape E = 40 cm² (10 × 4).
3 **81 m²** Calculate the area of the square and the rectangle separately, then add the answers together; 6 × 6 = 36 and 15 × 3 = 45; 36 + 45 = 81
4 **A and C, B and E** Shape A = 30 cm (9 + 6 = 15; 15 × 2 = 30); shape B = 28 cm (7 + 7 = 14; 14 × 2 = 28); shape C = 30 cm (7 + 8 = 15; 15 × 2 = 30); shape D = 26 cm (5 + 8 = 13; 13 × 2 = 26) and shape E = 28 cm (8 + 6 = 14; 14 × 2 = 28).

5 **57 cm²** Use column multiplication, ensuring the decimal point is lined up in the answer space. Work from left to right and add on any numbers carried over, as with other column multiplication equations.

```
        9 . 5
    ×       6
    ---------
        5 7 . 0
        5 3
```

6 **31 cm** Refer to Focus test 6 Q10 on adding decimal numbers; 9.5 + 6.0 = 15.5; 15.5 × 2 = 31
7 **420 cm²** Refer to Focus test 2 Q4 on long multiplication or page 6 on grid multiplication; 35 × 12 = 420
8 **94 cm** 35 + 12 = 47; 47 × 2 = 94
9 **4 cm** All sides on a square are equal, so the same number will be multiplied together to find the area (4 × 4 = 16); or divide the perimeter by the number of sides (16 ÷ 4 = 4).
10 **4500 m²** Refer to Focus test 1 Q5 on multiplying by 100; 45 × 100 = 4500
11 **42.25 cm²** To multiply two decimal numbers together, remove the decimal point and multiply as normal (refer to Focus test 2 Q4 on long multiplication); then count the number of digits after the decimal point in the original equation to find how many digits are after the decimal in the answer; 65 × 65 = 4225; in 6.5 × 6.5 there are 2 digits after the decimal point, so the answer is 42.25
12 **26 cm** 6.5 + 6.5 = 13; 13 × 2 = 26

Focus test 9 (pages 20–21)

1–5 Refer to Focus test 1 Q5 on multiplying and dividing by 10, 100 and 1000.

1

Metres	Centimetres	Millimetres
0.95 m	95 cm	950 mm
12.4 m	1240 cm	12 400 mm
6.8 m	680 cm	6800 mm

Multiply metres by 100 to find cm (0.95 m × 100 = 95 cm); multiply cm by 10 to find mm (1240 cm × 10 = 12 400 mm); divide cm by 100 to find metres (1240 cm ÷ 100 = 12.40) divide mm by 10 to find cm (6800 ÷ 10 = 680).

2 **8500 ml** 1 litre = 1000 ml, so multiply by 1000; 8.5 × 1000 = 8500
3 **4700 kg** 1 tonne = 1000 kg, so multiply by 1000; 4.7 × 1000 = 4700
4 **6.85 kg** 1 kg = 1000 g, so multiply the 6.85 kg by 1000 and compare; 6.85 × 1000 = 6850 g; 6850 > 690
5 **105 mm, 1.05 m, 150 cm, 1550 cm** Change the lengths so they are all shown in the same unit of measurement. For example, change them all into cm by multiplying those shown in metres by 100 (1.05 m × 100 = 105 cm) and dividing measurements shown in mm by 10 (105 mm ÷ 10 = 10.5 cm). Then place them in order: 10.5 cm, 105 cm, 150 cm, 1550 cm.

6–7 Refer to the table on imperial measurements on page 21 and Focus test 8 Q5 on multiplying decimal numbers.

6 **7 pints** 1.76 × 4 = 7.04 which is 7.00 when rounded.
7 **15 miles** 8 km × 3 = 24 km, so multiply 5 miles by 3 also to find 15.
8 **25 cm** 2.5 × 10 = 25
9 **450 ml** Find what the smaller lines between the measurements shown represent. The first jug has been separated into 5 equal parts between each 500 ml so each small line represents 100 ml and 1700 ml is shown. The second jug has been separated into $\frac{1}{4}$ litres (1 litre ÷ 4 = $\frac{1}{4}$ litre) so $1\frac{1}{4}$ litres is shown. Change the measurements into the same format; 1 litre = 1000 ml and 1000 ÷ 4 = 250 so $\frac{1}{4}$ litre = 250; 1000 + 250 = 1250; 1700 – 1250 = 450
10 **2.95 litres** 1700 + 1250 = 2950; then divide by 1000 to change to litres; 2950 ÷ 1000 = 2.950
11 **20:40** The time is 25 mins past so add 15 mins to 25; 15 + 25 = 40 so it will be 20:40. To change times shown in 24-hour clock to analogue, subtract 12 from the hours (20 – 12 = 8 so it is 8:40 p.m.). Moving around a clock face, each number represents 5 minutes that have passed. Use the numbers on the clock to count up in 5s: the minute hand points to 8 to show 40 mins; the hour hand is shown just before the 9 as the hour moves from 8 to 9.

12 **500 g** Refer to Q9 on reading scales; 1 kg = 1000 g and 1000 ÷ 4 = 250 so each small line represents 250 g; the first scale shows 750 g (500 + 250) and the second scale shows 1250 g (1000 + 250); the difference is 1250 – 750 = 500.

Focus test 10 (pages 22–23)

1–6 Refer to the explanation of coordinates on page 22.
1 **(−2, −3)**
2 **(−2, 4)**
3 **(2, 4)**
4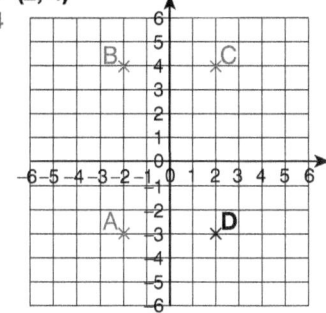

As it is a rectangle, opposite sides are equal in length; Point A is 7 squares below Point B, so Point D will be 7 squares below Point C.

5 **(2, −3)**
6 **(70, 10)** The bottom right corner of the triangle will be the same distance apart from the centre as the bottom left, so subtract 10 from 40 to find how far away from the middle it is (40 − 10 = 30) then add this to 40 to find the missing coordinate on the horizontal x-axis (40 + 30 = 70); the missing coordinate for the y-axis will be the same as it is level.

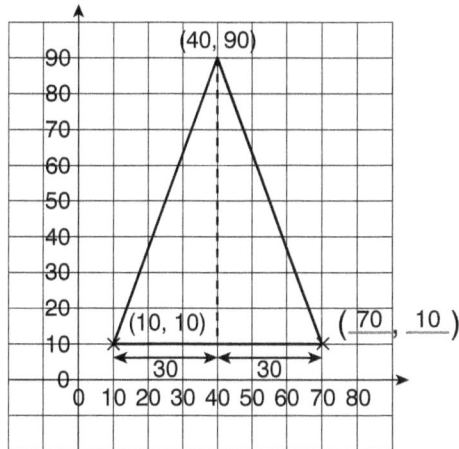

7 **rotated** The shape has been rotated 90° clockwise.
8 **translated** The shape has just been moved across the grid.
9 **reflected** A mirror image of the shape is shown.
10–12 Refer to the explanation of coordinates on page 22.

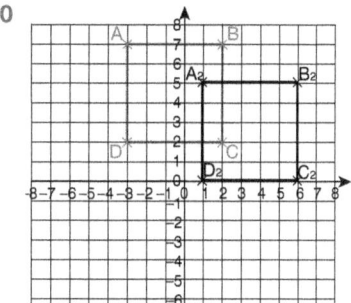

Point B has moved from (2, 7) to (6, 5) so the shape has moved **4** squares across (2 + **4** = 6) and **2** squares down (7 − **2** = 5), so all the other points will move in the same way.
11–12 A_2 **(1, 5)** C_2 **(6, 0)**

Focus test 11 (pages 24–25)

1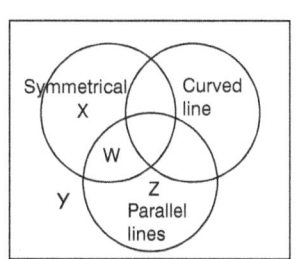

Refer to Focus test 7 Q2 and 3 on parallel lines and symmetry. 'X' is only symmetrical, so it is in the 'Symmetrical' set and does not overlap the others; 'W' is symmetrical and has parallel lines, so it is placed where only the 'Symmetrical' and 'Parallel lines' sets overlap; 'Z' only has parallel lines, so it is placed in the part of the 'Parallel lines' set where it does not overlap the others; '*Y*' is shown in the outside set as it is not symmetrical and has no curved or parallel lines.

2 **5** B, C, D, O and U are placed in the section where the 'Symmetrical' and 'Curved lines' sets overlap.
3 **12** L, K, N, F, R, G, P, S, Q, J, Z and *Y* are not in the 'Symmetrical' set.
4 **0** No letters are in the section where only the 'Parallel Lines' and 'Curved lines' sets overlap.
5 **U** Only U is in the section where all three sets intersect.
6 **K, L, *Y*** Only K, L and *Y* are placed in the outside set.
7–9 Refer to the explanation of reading graphs on page 25; each vertical line represents 2 letters. Look to see which numbers the grey bars are level with.

7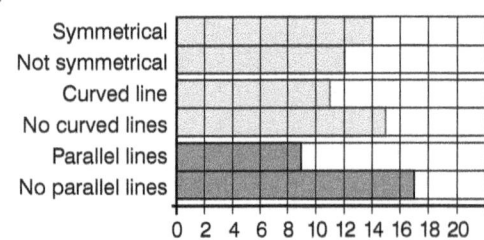

9 letters have parallel lines (E, I, M, H, U, N, F, W, Z); 17 letters do not have parallel lines (L, K, V, A, T, O, C, B, D, R, G, S, P, J, Q, Y, X).

8 **14** The grey bar showing symmetrical letters is level with 14.

9 **11** The grey bar showing curved letters is halfway between 10 and 12 so it represents 11.

10 $\frac{3}{8}$ 3 out of 8 sections show 'Non-fiction' books, so it is $\frac{3}{8}$.

11 **50%** Refer to the explanation of changing fractions into percentages on page 10; exactly $\frac{1}{2}$ of the pie chart shows 'Fiction'; $\frac{1}{2} = \frac{50}{100} = 50\%$

12 **5** 40 books ÷ 8 sections = 5 books per section; only 1 section shows 'Poetry'.

Focus test 12 (pages 26–27)

1–8 Refer to the explanation of mean, median, mode and range on page 26.

1 **10 cm** 11 + 11 + 10 + 14 + 7 + 9 + 8 = 70; 70 ÷ 7 = 10

2 **10 cm** 7, 8 , 9, 10, 11, 11, 14; the number in the middle is 10.

3 **11 cm** 11 cm occurs most often.

4 **7 cm** 14 − 7 = 7

5 **9 cm** 5 + 6 + 11 + 11 + 10 + 14 + 7 + 9 + 8 = 81; 81 ÷ 9 = 9

6 **9 cm** 5, 6, 7, 8 , 9, 10, 11, 11, 14; the number in the middle is 9.

7 **11 cm** 11 is still the number that occurs most often.

8 **9 cm** 14 − 5 = 9

9–12 Refer to Focus test 4 Q1–4 on simplifying fractions.

9 $\frac{1}{2}$ 4 out of 8 numbers are even so it is $\frac{4}{8}$ and $\frac{4}{8} = \frac{1}{2}$.

10 $\frac{1}{4}$ There are 2 multiples of 3 (3 and 6) out of 8 sections so it is $\frac{2}{8}$ and $\frac{2}{8} = \frac{1}{4}$.

11 $\frac{3}{4}$ 6 numbers that are less than 7 so it is $\frac{6}{8}$ and $\frac{6}{8} = \frac{3}{4}$.

12 $\frac{1}{8}$ Number 1 only appears 1 time out of 8 sections, so it is $\frac{1}{8}$.

Mixed paper 1 (pages 28–31)

1–3 Refer to Focus test 1 Q5 on multiplying by 1000.

1 **8200**

2 **6750**

3 **91 000**

4 **<** < means less than and > means greater than; refer to Focus test 1 Q7 on comparing decimal numbers and look at the digits in each column until one is found that is larger or smaller than the other.

5 **20.1 kg** Refer to Focus test 6 Q10 on adding decimal numbers; 14.6 + 5.5 = 20.1

6 **404 km** 483 − 79 = 404

7–9 Refer to Focus test 2 Q7–12 on division.

7 **56 r 3**

8 **26 r 3**

9 **65**

10 **144** Refer to Focus test 2 Q1–3 on column multiplication.

11–12 **(1, 45) (3, 15) (5, 9)** Refer to the explanation of factors on page 8; 3 × 15 = 45; 5 × 9 = 45

13–14 **48, 24** Refer to the explanation of multiples on page 9; find the multiples of 8 first (as it is the larger number there will be fewer); then find which of them can be divided exactly by 3; 16, 32, 48 and 24 are all multiples of 8; 48 ÷ 3 = 16 and 24 ÷ 3 = 8.

15–16 Refer to the explanation of changing fractions into percentages on page 10.

15 **90%** $\frac{45}{50} = \frac{90}{100} = 90\%$

16 **64%** $\frac{32}{50} = \frac{64}{100} = 64\%$

17 **0.5 (or 0.50)** Write the numbers in the percentage as the 2 digits after the decimal point; 0.50 is the same as 0.5.

18 **0.25** $\frac{1}{4} = \frac{25}{100}$ as 1 × 25 = 25 and 4 × 25 = 100 (refer to page 10 on equivalent fractions); when a fraction has a denominator of 100, the numerator can be written after the decimal point, so $\frac{25}{100} = 0.25$.

19–22 Refer to Focus test 5 Q1–3 on sequences.

19 **−6** 4 − 2 = 2; the numbers decrease so the rule is 'subtract 2'; 2 subtracted from −4 = −6.

20 **5** 3 is the same as 3.0 and 3.0 − 2.5 = 0.5; the numbers increase so the rule is 'add 0.5'; 4.5 + 0.5 = 5.0

21 **267** 767 − 667 = 100; the numbers decrease so the rule is 'subtract 100'; 367 − 100 = 267

22 **49** The numbers increase but addition does not work, so it must be multiplication; 2 × 2 = 4; 3 × 3 = 9 so it is a sequence of square numbers; 7 × 7 = 49

23–25

Pile	1	2	3	4
Number of bricks	3	6	10	15

26 **21** 1 more brick is added to the number of bricks in the previous row each time; 5 + 1 = 6; 15 + 6 = 21

27 **hexagon** A 6-sided shape is a hexagon.

28 **6** Refer to Focus test 7 Q3 on symmetry.

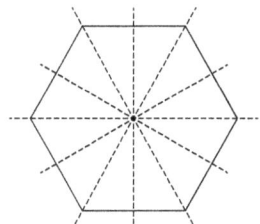

29 **obtuse** Obtuse angles are between 90° and 180°.

30 **3** Refer to Focus test 7 Q2 on parallel lines.

31–34 Refer to the explanations of area and perimeter on pages 18–19 and Focus test 2 Q1–3 on column multiplication.

31 **B and D** Shape A = 84 cm² (6 × 14), shape B = 60 cm² (12 × 5), shape C = 48 cm² (16 × 3), shape D = 60 cm² (4 × 15).

32 **C and D** Shape A = 40 cm (6 + 14 = 20; 20 × 2 = 40); shape B = 34 cm (12 + 5 = 17; 17 × 2 = 34); shape C = 38 cm (16 + 3 = 19; 19 × 2 = 38); shape D = 38 cm (4 + 15 = 19; 19 × 2 = 38). In fact, it is only necessary to add the two given sides for each shape to find the two which are the same.

33 **9 cm** Use knowledge of times tables; 7 × 9 = 63

34 **68 m²** Find the area of each rectangle, then add the answers; 4 × 7 = 28 and 8 × 5 = 40; 28 + 40 = 68

35 **32 mm** 1 cm = 10 mm; the line is level with 2 mm after 3 cm (which is 30 mm); 30 mm + 2 mm = 32 mm.

36 **3.4 kg** The scale has been separated into 10 equal parts between every 1 kg and 1 ÷ 10 = 0.1 (refer to Focus test 1 Q5 on dividing by 10); the arrow points to the fourth line after 3 kg so it is 3.4.

37–38 1000 ml = 1 litre and 1000 g = 1 kg, so multiply the litres and kg by 1000 then compare (refer to Focus test 1 Q5 on multiplying by 1000).

37 **=** 1.7 × 1000 = 1700

38 **>** 4.5 × 1000 = 4500; 4500 > 450

39–41 Refer to the explanation of coordinates on page 22.

39 **(3, 1)**

40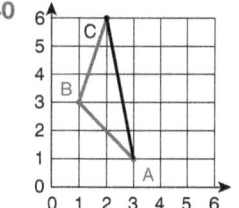

41 **(2, 3)**

42 A translated shape is moved without being rotated or reflected.

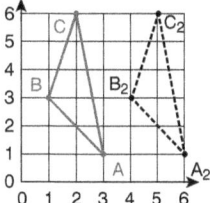

43–46 To read a bar chart, look at the number each bar is level with. The graph has been separated into 2 equal parts between every 10 children, so each horizontal line represents 5 children (as 10 ÷ 2 = 5).

43 **141–150 cm** The highest bar is shown for 141–150 cm.

44 **40** 30 were 151–160 cm and 10 were over 160 cm; 30 + 10 = 40

45 **30** 35 were 131–140 cm and 5 were 130 or under; 35 – 5 = 30

46 **151–160 cm** It is not more than 160 so it is included in the range of 151–160 cm.

47–50 Refer to the explanation of mean, median, mode and range on page 26.

47 **5p** There are more 5ps than any other coin.

48 **15p** 1 + 50 + 5 + 20 + 50 + 2 + 10 + 5 + 5 + 2 = 150; 150 ÷ 10 = 15

49 **5p** 1, 2, 2, 5, 5, 5, 10, 20, 50, 50; the number in the middle is 5.

50 **49p** 50 – 1 = 49

Mixed paper 2 (pages 32–34)

1–2 Refer to Focus test 1 Q4 on rounding. When rounded to the nearest whole, the number in the ones place is rounded to.

1 **840 m** 9 is in the ones place and 5 is to its right, so 9 increases; as 10 is 1 more than 9, the 9 changes to 0 and the 3 in the tens place increases by 1.

2 **107 m** 7 is in the ones place and 4 is to its right, so 7 remains the same.

3–4 Refer to Focus test 1 Q5 on dividing by 100.

3 **8.26**   4 **10.95**

5–6 Refer to Focus test 5 Q1 on subtracting decimal numbers.

5 **44.1**   6 **60.4**

7–10 Refer to Focus test 2 Q1–3 and Q7–12 on column multiplication and division.

7 **8000** Another approach to this is to remove the zeros from both numbers and multiply (2 × 4 = 8), then count the zeros in the original equation to find how many should be in the answer; there are 3 zeros in 20 × 400 so it is 8000.

8 **168** 9 **28** 10 **43**

11–14 Refer to the explanation of factors and multiples on pages 8 and 9.

11–12 **96, 24** 12 × 8 = **96**; 3 × 8 = **24**

13 **True** 17 × 4 = 68

14 **False** 12 × 6 = 72, so 6 cannot be multiplied to give an answer of 74.

15–16 < means less than and > means greater than. Find equivalent fractions with the same denominator by multiplying the numerator (top number) and denominator (bottom number) by the same number, then compare.

15 < $\frac{4}{5} = \frac{8}{10}$ (as 4 × 2 = 8 and 5 × 2 = 10); $\frac{8}{10} < \frac{9}{10}$

16 > $\frac{3}{4} = \frac{9}{12}$ (as 3 × 3 = 9 and 4 × 3 = 12); $\frac{2}{3} = \frac{8}{12}$ (as 2 × 4 = 8 and 3 × 4 = 12); $\frac{9}{12} > \frac{8}{12}$

17 **20** To find a fraction of a number, divide the number by the denominator then multiply by the numerator; 30 ÷ 3 = 10 and 10 × 2 = 20 so $\frac{2}{3}$ of 30 = 20.

18 **15** The number of spoons of fruit has been multiplied by 3, so multiply the spoons of yoghurt by 3 also; 3 × 5 = 15

19–22 Refer to Focus test 5 Q1–3 on sequences.

19–20 **4, 128** The numbers increase, so it is addition or multiplication and both work for this sequence; the rule is 'add multiples of 8' (+ 8, + 16, + 32 and so on) or 'multiply by 2' (8 × 2 = 16, 16 × 2 = 32 and so on).

21–22 **308, 558** 408 − 358 = 50; the numbers increase, so the rule is 'add 50'; 308 + 50 = 358; 508 + 50 = 558

23–26 Refer to Focus test 6 Q1–6 on completing the inverse.

23 **8** 31 − 23 = 8

24 **36** 9 × 4 = 36

25 **57** 32 + 25 = 57

26 **9** 45 ÷ 5 = 9

27–29 **Faces = 4, Edges = 6, Vertices = 4** Refer to Focus test 7 Q8 on edges, faces and vertices of a shape. A tetrahedron is a triangular-based pyramid, as shown.

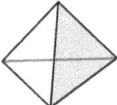

30 **Angle x = 130°** Refer to Focus test 7 Q12 on using a protractor.

31–34 Refer to the explanations of area and perimeter on pages 18–19 and Focus test 2 Q1–3 on column multiplication.

31 **70 cm²** 14 × 5 = 70

32 **38 cm** 14 + 5 = 19; 19 × 2 = 38

33 **81 cm²** As the shape is a square, all sides are the same length; 9 × 9 = 81

34 **36 cm** 9 + 9 = 18; 18 × 2 = 36

35–36 Between each of the larger lines, the scale has been separated into 10 equal parts, so each small line represents 1° (10 ÷ 10 = 1). Find the number the grey line is level with.

35 **12°C** 36 **−5°C**

37 **1 hr 35 min** Use a number line to calculate the elapsed time, as shown; 1 hr = 60 mins and 95 − 60 = 35, so 95 mins = 1 hr 35 mins

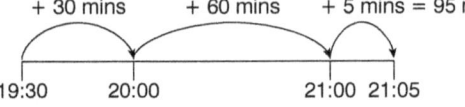

38 **3700 g** 1 kg = 1000 g, so multiply by 1000; 3.7 × 1000 = 3700 (refer to Focus test 1 Q5 on multiplying by 1000).

39–41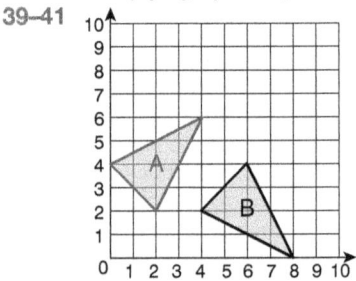

Refer to the explanation of coordinates on page 22.

42 **rotation** Refer to the explanation of transformations on page 23.

43 $\frac{3}{10}$ 3 out of 10 segments represent vans, so it is $\frac{3}{10}$.

44 **10%** Refer to the explanation of changing fractions into percentages on page 10; $\frac{1}{10}$ were bicycles; $\frac{1}{10} = \frac{10}{100} = 10\%$.

45 **80** The pie chart is separated into 10 equal segments and 200 ÷ 10 = 20 so each segment represents 20 vehicles; 4 segments are shown for the cars and 4 × 20 = 80.

46 **20** 3 × 20 = 60 vans; 2 × 20 = 40 lorries; 60 − 40 = 20. Another approach is each of the segments = 20 vehicles (200 ÷ 10) and there is one more segment of vans than lorries.

47 **unlikely** There is a less than even chance of seeing a hot air balloon, but it is not impossible so it is 'unlikely'.
48 **impossible** The sun will never shine at midnight (in the UK), so this is 'impossible'.
49 **certain** A person is unable not to blink for a whole day, so it is 'certain'.
50 **likely** It is not absolutely certain, but a greater than even chance, so it is 'likely'.

Mixed paper 3 (pages 35–38)

1 **10 g** Refer to Focus test 1 Q4 on rounding; 1 plum = 58 g which is 60 g when rounded to the nearest 10.
2–3 **9.299**, **29.3** Refer to Focus test 1 Q7 on comparing decimal numbers; to find the smallest number, look for the smallest digit in each column.
4 **£147** Refer to Focus test 1 Q4 on rounding; 6 is in the pounds place, 5 is to its right so the 6 increases by 1; money is always written with 2 digits after the decimal, so change the digit in the 1ps place to 0.
5–6 < means less than and > means greater than.
5 < 54 + 17 = 71 and 123 − 51 = 72; 71 < 72
6 < 140 − 84 = 56 and 27 + 33 = 60; 56 < 60.

7–10
IN	270	**150**	300	**240**	600
OUP	9	5	**10**	8	**20**

Divide each number in the top row by 30 to find the number missing beneath it; multiply each number in the bottom row by 30 to find the number missing above it; 5 × 30 = **150**; 300 ÷ 30 = **10**; 8 × 30 = **240**; 600 ÷ 30 = **20**

11–14 Refer to the explanations of factors and prime numbers on page 8; a square number is the answer when a number is multiplied by itself (e.g. 5 × 5 = 25).
11–12 **4 and 9** 4 × 9 = 36
13 **29** 29 is the next number that has only 2 factors (1 and 29).
14 **20** 10^2 = 100 and $\sqrt{25}$ is the square root of 25, which is 5 (as 5 × 5 = 25); 100 ÷ 5 = 20
15 **1 : 3** There are 4 black tiles to 12 grey tiles, so it is 4 : 12 which can be simplified to 1 : 3 as both numbers can be divided by 4 (4 ÷ 4 = 1; 12 ÷ 4 = 3).
16–17 **Black → 20 tiles, Grey → 60 tiles** The ratio is 1 : 3 (see Q15) which is 4 tiles altogether (1 black + 3 grey) so divide 80 by 4 then multiply by each number in the ratio by the answer; 80 ÷ 4 = 20; 1 × 20 = 20 black tiles and 3 × 20 = 60 grey tiles.

18 $\frac{5}{15}$ Simplify each fraction wherever possible (refer to Focus test 4 Q1–4 on simplifying fractions); only $\frac{1}{15}$ simplifies to $\frac{1}{3}$.
19 **34** Refer to Q14 on square numbers; 3^2 = 9 and 5^2 = 25; 9 + 25 = 34
20–22 Refer to Focus test 5 Q1–3 on sequences.
20 **28** 20 − 12 = 8; the numbers increase, so the rule is 'add 8'; 20 + 8 = 28
21 **139** 145 − 142 = 3; the numbers decrease, so the rule is 'subtract 3'; 142 − 3 = 139
22 **450** 300 − 150 = 150; the numbers increase, so the rule is 'add 150'; 300 + 150 = 450
23 **28** 23 + 5 = 28
24 **20** 4r = 4 × r; 4 × 5 = 20
25–26 Refer to Focus test 6 Q1–6 on completing the inverse.
25 **9** 34 − 25 = 9
26 **3** 6b = 6 × b; 18 ÷ 6 = 3
27–30 Refer to Focus test 7 Q2 and Q3 on parallel lines and symmetry. Perpendicular lines are at right angles to one another.
27 Line ED (or DE)   28 Line CD (or DC)
29 **acute** An acute angle is less than 90°.
30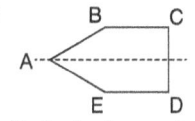

31–34 Refer to the explanations of area and perimeter on pages 18–19; all 4 sides on a square are equal length.
31 **121 cm²** 11 × 11 = 121
32 **44 cm** 11 × 2 = 22; 22 × 2 = 44
33 **Check a square 5 grid squares × 5 grid squares is drawn, e.g.**

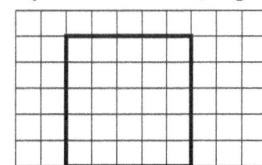

The same number will be multiplied together to make 25; 5 × 5 = 25, so each side is 5 cm.
34 **20 cm** 5 + 5 = 10; 10 × 2 = 20
35 **1.2 litres** The scale has been separated into 10 equal parts between every 1 litre and 1 ÷ 10 = 0.1 (refer to Focus test 1 Q5 on dividing by 10); the grey shaded area is level with 1.2.
36 **800 ml** 1 litre = 1000 ml, so multiply 1.2 by 1000 (refer to Focus test 1 Q5 on multiplying by 1000) and subtract 400; 1.2 × 1000 = 1200; 1200 − 400 = 800
37 **8:35 a.m.** Refer to Focus test 9 Q11 on telling the time. The time shown is 8:10; 10 mins + 25 mins = 35 mins, so it will be 8:35.

38 **2:55 p.m.** Count back to 3:00 by subtracting 20 mins; 25 − 20 = 5 mins left to subtract; 5 mins before 3:00 is 2:55.

39–40 Refer to the explanation of transformations on page 23.

39 **reflection**   40 **rotation**

41–42 **(3, 4), (−4, 3)** Refer to the explanation of coordinates on page 22.

43–46 A square number is the answer when a number has been multiplied by itself (e.g. 5 × 5 = 25), even numbers can be divided exactly by 2 and a multiple of 3 is the answer when a number has been multiplied by 3.

43–44
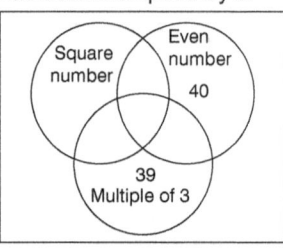

39 is only a multiple of 3 (13 × 3 = 39), so it is placed in the 'Multiple of 3' set where it does not overlap the others; 40 is only an even number, so it is placed in the 'Even Number' set where it does not overlap the others.

45 **36** Only 36 is in the section where the 3 sets overlap.

46 **13** Count all the numbers in the whole of the 'Multiple of 3' set.

47–50 Refer to the explanation of mean, median, mode and range on page 26.

47 **17** 17 + 18 + 15 + 20 + 15 = 85; 85 ÷ 5 = 17

48 **17** 15, 15, 17, 18, 20; the middle number is 17.

49 **15** 15 occurs the most often.

50 **5** 20 − 15 = 5

Mixed paper 4 (pages 38–41)

1 **753 006** Refer to Focus test 1 Q1 on writing numbers using a place value grid; 752 906 + 100 = 753 006

2 **751 906** 2 is in the thousands place, so decrease this digit by 1.

3 **753 000** Refer to Focus test 1 Q4 on rounding; 2 is in the thousands place and 9 is to its right, so 2 increases by 1.

4 **753 906** 2 is in the thousands place, so increase this digit by 1.

5 **£193.97** Refer to Focus test 8 Q5 on multiplying decimal numbers and Focus test 6 Q10 on adding decimal numbers; 39.49 × 2 = 78.98; 78.98 + 114.99 = 193.97

6 **£6.03** Refer to Focus test 5 Q1–3 on subtracting decimal numbers; 200.00 − 193.97 = 6.03

7 **7110** Refer to page 6 and Focus test 2 Q7 on multiplying using a grid.

8–9 Refer to Focus test 2 Q1–3 on column multiplication.

8 **2776**   9 **1872**

10 **14 r 1** Refer to Focus test 2 Q7–12 on division.

11–12 < means less than and > means greater than; the square root sign (√) is used to show the answer to a number that has been multiplied by itself.

11 **=** 3^2 = 3 × 3 which is 9; √81 = 9 as 9 × 9 = 81.

12 **<** √144 = 12 as 12 × 12 = 144; 4^2 = 4 × 4 which is 16; 12 < 16

13–14 **37, 29** Refer to the explanation of prime numbers on page 8.

15 $\frac{1}{3}$ 4 out of 12 are green which is $\frac{4}{12}$ and this can be simplified to $\frac{1}{3}$ (refer to Focus test 4 Q1–4 on simplifying fractions).

16 **50%** Refer to the explanations of equivalent fractions changing fractions into percentages on page 10; $\frac{6}{12} = \frac{1}{2}$; $\frac{50}{100}$ is the equivalent of $\frac{1}{2}$; $\frac{50}{500} = 50\%$

17–18 **0.4, 5%** $\frac{1}{2} = \frac{50}{100}$ which is the same as 0.50 (or 0.5) and 50%, so look for percentages or decimals less than 0.5 or 50%; in fractions that are equivalent to $\frac{1}{2}$ the numerator (top number) is always exactly half of the denominator (bottom number), e.g. $\frac{4}{8}$ and $\frac{5}{10}$ are both equal to $\frac{1}{2}$, so $\frac{3}{5}$ and $\frac{6}{10}$ are larger.

19–22 Refer to Focus test 5 Q1–3 on sequences.

19–20 **9, 4** Use knowledge of times tables (7 × 7 = **49**; 6 × 6 = **36**; 5 × 5 = **25** and so on); 3 × 3 = **9** and 2 × 2 = **4**. This sequence is the square numbers.

21–22 **481, 479** 489 − 487 = 2; the numbers decrease so the rule is 'subtract 2'; 483 − 2 = 481; 481 − 2 = 479

23–24 Refer to Focus test 6 Q1–6 on completing the inverse.

23 **54** 70 − 16 = 54

24 **9** 3n = 3 × n; 27 ÷ 3 = 9

25–26 **18 cups of flour, 6 eggs** Multiply the amounts shown for 10 biscuits by 3 to find how much is needed for 30; 6 × 3 = 18; 2 × 3 = 6

27–30

	Pyramid	Prism
Shape letter	B C	A D

A pyramid has a base and all the sides connected to the base rise to meet in a point. Prisms are shapes with two identical faces at each end (referred to as the 'end face'). If the end of a prism were 'sliced off', the end face will always remain the same.

31–34 Refer to the explanations of area and perimeter on pages 18–19 and Focus test 2 Q1–3 on column multiplication.
31 **225 cm²** 25 × 9 = 225
32 **68 cm** 25 + 9 = 34; 34 × 2 = 68
33 **144 cm²** 12 × 12 = 144
34 **48 cm** 12 + 12 = 24; 24 × 2 = 48
35–38 Refer to Focus test 1 Q5 on multiplying and dividing by 10, 100 and 1000.
35 **67 cm** 10 mm = 1 cm, so divide by 10; 670 ÷ 10 = 67
36 **900 ml** 1 litre = 1000 ml, so multiply by 1000; 0.9 × 1000 = 900
37 **840 cm** 1 m = 100 cm, so multiply by 100; 8.4 × 100 = 840
38 **3.8 kg** 1000 g = 1 kg, so divide by 1000; 3800 ÷ 1000 = 3.8
39–41 Refer to the explanation of coordinates on page 22.
39 **(–2, 1)**
40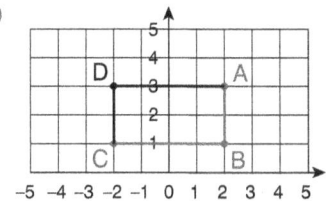
As it is a rectangle, opposite sides are equal length; Point A is 2 squares above Point B, so Point D will be 2 squares above Point C also.
41 **(–2, 3)**
42 **flag c** Refer to the explanation of transformations on page 23; flag a is a reflection, flag b is a reflection and has been rotated 180°, flag c has been rotated 180°.
43–46 To read a conversion chart, find the given measurement on the chart and use a ruler to draw a line that meets the diagonal line, as shown for question 43 below (A). Draw another line (B) from that point to find the number along the other axis it is level with.

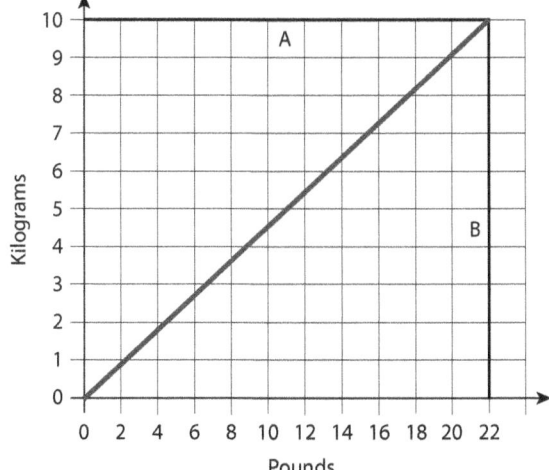

43 **22 lb** The part of the diagonal line 10 kg crosses is level with 22 pounds.
44 **5 kg** Place the ruler vertically half way between 10 and 12 pounds; the part of the diagonal line it crosses is level with 5 kg.
45 **1 kg** The part of the diagonal line 2 pounds crosses is level with is just below 1 kg.
46 **6 kilograms** The part of the diagonal line 6 kg crosses is level with approximately 13 pounds; 13 pounds > 6 pounds
47 **even chance** There are an equal number of odd and even numbers on fair dice, so it is an 'even chance'.
48 **unlikely** Only 1 side out of 6 has the number 1 on, so it is 'unlikely'.
49 **unlikely** Only 2 sides out of 6 have multiples of 3 (3 and 6) so it is 'unlikely'.
50 **impossible** 7 is not on fair dice, so it is 'impossible'.

Mixed paper 5 (pages 42–46)

1–2 Refer to Focus test 1 Q4 on rounding.
1 **26.5** 5 is in the tenths place and 0 is to its right, so 5 remains the same.
2 **349.1** 0 is in the tenths place and 6 is to its right, so 0 increases by 1.
3–4 **5.03, 5.77** The number line has been separated into 10 equal parts between 5 and 6 so each one represents 0.1 (as 6 – 5 = 1 and 1 ÷ 10 = 0.1). It is separated into a further 10 equal parts between each of the larger lines, therefore each small line represents 0.01 (as 0.1 ÷ 10 = 0.01). Remember decimal numbers increase in the same way as whole numbers, e.g. 5.09, 5.10, 5.11, 5.12 and so on.
5 **7352** 5406 + 1946 = 7352
6 **3422** 7200 – 3778 = 3422
7 **1794** Refer to Focus test 2 Q6 on multiplying using a grid.
8 **5** 5 × 12 = 60 so 10 eggs will be left over.
9 **£240** 4 × 6 = 24, so 4 × 60 = 240
10 **12** 32 × 3 books = 96 books needed; 96 ÷ 8 = 12
11–14 Refer to the explanation of factors and prime numbers on page 8.
11 **3** 3 × 4 = 12; 3 × 9 = 27
12 **always** A prime number only has 2 factors, so will always have an even number.
13 **never** A square number is the answer when a number is multiplied by itself (e.g. 5 × 5 = 25) and this number only needs to be written once (e.g. factors of 25 are 1, 5 and 25), so it will never have an even number.
14 **9** The factors of 18 are: 1, 2, 3, 6, 9, 18.
15–16 Refer to Focus test 4 Q1–4 on finding a fraction shown on a shape and simplifying and to changing fractions into percentages on page 10.

15 $\frac{3}{5}$ $\frac{6}{10} = \frac{3}{5}$

16 **40%** $\frac{4}{10} = \frac{40}{100} = 40\%$.

17–18 < means less than and > means greater than; refer to Focus test 1 Q7 on comparing decimal numbers and look at the digits in each column until one is found that is larger or smaller than the other.

17 **>**

18 **<**

19–22 Refer to Focus test 5 Q1–3 on sequences.

19 **6.5** 5.0 − 4.5 = 0.5; the numbers increase so the rule is 'add 0.5'; 6.0 + 0.5 = 6.5

20 **2$\frac{1}{4}$** $1\frac{1}{4} + \frac{1}{4} = 1\frac{1}{2}$ so the rule is 'add $\frac{1}{4}$'; $2 + \frac{1}{4} = 2\frac{1}{4}$

21 **0** 12 − 9 = 3; the numbers decrease so the rule is 'subtract 3'; 3 − 3 = 0

22 **−30** Refer to Focus test 5 Q3 on negative numbers; 10 − 0 = 10 so the rule is 'subtract 10'; 10 subtracted from −20 = −30.

23 **11** 5h = 35 (5 × 7) and 3k = 24 (3 × 8); 35 − 24 = 11

24 **37** 3h = 21 (3 × 7) and 2k = 16 (2 × 8); 21 + 16 = 37

25–26 Refer to Focus test 6 Q1–6 on completing the inverse.

25 **27** 56 − 29 = 27

26 **9** 81 ÷ 9 = 9

27 **False** Refer to Focus test 7 Q2 on parallel lines.

28 **Angle d = 130°** Refer to page 17: angles in a quadrilateral add up to 360°; 50° + 90° + 90° = 230°; 360° − 230° = 130°.

29 **trapezium** A trapezium is a quadrilateral with only 2 sides that are parallel.

30 **4** A square-based pyramid is being described.

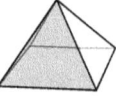

31–34 Refer to the explanations of area and perimeter on pages 18–19 and Focus test 2 Q1–3 on column multiplication.

31 **114 cm²** 19 × 6 = 114

32 **120 cm²** 15 × 8 = 120

33 **A** Shape A = 50 cm (19 + 6 = 25; 25 × 2); shape B = 46 cm (15 + 8 = 23; 23 × 2); 50 > 46

34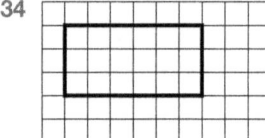

Half of 18 = 9 so 2 different sides of the rectangle will add up to 9 cm; find 2 numbers that add up to 9 and can be multiplied together to make 18; 3 + 6 = 9 and 3 × 6 = 18.

35 **2 litres** 5 × 400 = 2000; 1000 ml = 1 litre so 2000 ml = 2 litres.

36 **2 m** Refer to the table on imperial measurements on page 21; 1 m ≈ 3 feet, so 2 m ≈ 6 feet. (The ≈ symbol means 'approximately equal to'.)

37 **750 g** Refer to Focus test 9 Q9 on reading scales; 1 kg = 1000 g and 1000 ÷ 4 = 250 so each small line represents 250 g; the first scale shows 500 g and the second scale shows 1250 g (1000 + 250); 1250 − 500 = 750

38 **1.75 kg** 500 + 1250 = 1750; 1 kg = 1000 g so divide by 1000; 1750 ÷ 1000 = 1.750 (refer to Focus test 1 Q5 on dividing by 1000)

39–41 Refer to the explanation of transformations on page 23.

39 **translation**

40 **reflection**

41 **rotation**

42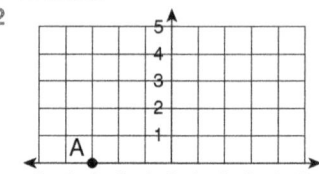

Refer to the explanation of coordinates on page 22.

43–46 Refer to the explanation of reading graphs on page 25; between every 50 litres, the chart has been separated into 10 equal parts, so each vertical line represents 5 litres (as 50 ÷ 10 = 5). Look to see which numbers the grey bars are level with.

43 **Washing clothes** The grey bar for 'Washing clothes' is level with 90.

44 **60 litres** The grey bar for 'Outdoors' is level with 60.

45 **30 litres** The grey bar for 'Drinking, cooking and washing up' is level with 120; 120 − 90 = 30

46 **330 litres** The grey bar for 'Flushing toilets' is level with 180; the grey bar for 'Baths and showers' is level with 150; 180 + 150 = 330

47–50 Refer to the explanation of mean, median, mode and range on page 26.

47 **50 g** 55 + 40 + 35 + 55 + 80 + 40 + 55 + 40 + 40 = 450; 450 ÷ 9 = 50

48 **45 g** 40, 40, 40, 40, 45, 55, 55, 55, 80; the number in the middle is 45.

49 **40 g** 40 occurs most often.

50 **40 g** 80 − 40 = 40

Mixed paper 6 (pages 47–51)

1–4

Metres	Centimetres	Millimetres
6.4 m	**640 cm**	**6400 mm**
5.01 m	**501 cm**	**5010 mm**

Refer to Focus test 1 Q5 on multiplying and dividing by 10, 100 and 1000; multiply metres by 100 to find cm, then multiply cm by 10 to find mm.

5–6 Work from right to left, as when completing other column additions and think of the equation in each column as a missing number sentence to help. Also consider if any digits have been carried over. In the first column, 9 + 1 = 10 so 1 is carried over; 8 + **7** + 1 = 16 and 1 is carried over; **5** + 2 + 1 = 8

```
    5  8  1
+   2  7  9
   -------
    8  6  0
    1  1
```

7–10 < means less than and > means greater than. Refer to Focus test 2 Q1–3 and Q7 on column multiplication and division.

- 7 **=** 19 × 6 = 114 and 3 × 38 = 114
- 8 **<** 72 ÷ 4 = 18 and 57 ÷ 3 = 19; 18 < 19
- 9 **78** 546 ÷ 7 = 78
- 10 **96** 768 ÷ 8 = 96

11–13 **1, 2, 7 and 14** Refer to the explanation of factors on page 8; **1** × 28 = 28 and **2** × **14** = 28; **1** × 70 = 70, **2** × 35 = 70; **7** × 10 = 70

- 14 **17** Refer to the explanation of prime numbers on page 8; 4^2 = 16 (as 4 × 4 = 16) so 17 is closest.
- 15 **15** To find a fraction of a number, divide the number by the denominator then multiply by the numerator; 20 ÷ 4 = 5; 5 × 3 = 15 so $\frac{3}{4}$ of 20 = 15.

16–17 Refer to the explanation of equivalent fractions on page 10; look at the number shown in the second fraction to find what to multiply the other number multiply by.

- 16 $\frac{10}{20}$ 1 × 10 = 10; 2 × 10 = 20
- 17 $\frac{8}{10}$ 5 × 2 = 10; 4 × 2 = 8
- 18 **20%** Refer to the explanation of changing fractions into percentages on page 10; $\frac{10}{50}$ are broken (as it is 10 out of 50); $\frac{10}{50} = \frac{20}{100}$ = 20%.

19–22 Refer to Focus test 5 Q1–3 on sequences.

19–20 **4715, 4775** 4745 – 4730 = 15; the numbers increase so the rule is 'add 15'; **4715** + 15 = 4730; 4760 + 15 = **4775**

21–22 **0.2, 1 (or 1.0)** 0.6 – 0.4 = 0.2; the numbers increase so the rule is 'add 0.2'; 0.2 + 0.2 = 0.4; 0.8 + 0.2 = 1.0

23–26 Refer to Focus test 6 Q1–6 on completing the inverse.

- 23 **5** 10 + 10 = 20 so 4q = 20; 20 ÷ 4 = 5
- 24 **2** 10 – 4 = 6 so 3p = 6; 6 ÷ 3 = 2
- 25 **2** 4 + 2 = 6 so 3y = 6; 6 ÷ 3 = 2
- 26 **4** 9 – 1 = 8 so 2y = 8; 8 ÷ 2 = 4

27–28 Angles in a triangle always add up to 180°.

- 27 **30°** 60° + 90° = 150°; 180° – 150° = 30°
- 28 **60°** 40° + 80° = 120°; 180° – 120° = 60°

29–30 **3 rectangles, 2 triangles**

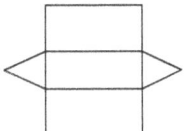

31–34 Refer to the explanations of area and perimeter on pages 18–19.

- 31 **54 m** 18 + 9 = 27; 27 × 2 = 54
- 32 **A and B have the same area.** 12 × 6 = 72; 8 × 9 = 72
- 33 **2 m** Shape A = 36 m (12 + 6 = 18; 18 × 2 = 36); Shape B = 34 m (8 + 9 = 17; 17 × 2 = 34); 36 – 34 = 2
- 34 **7.5 m²** Refer to Focus test 8 Q5 on multiplying decimal numbers; 2.5 × 3 = 7.5

35–38 As there are 12 shapes, write the fraction with a denominator of 12 to begin with, then simplify (refer to Focus test 4 Q1–4 on simplifying fractions).

- 35 $\frac{1}{4}$ 3 out of 12 are circles; $\frac{3}{50} = \frac{1}{4}$
- 36 $\frac{1}{2}$ 6 out of 12 are quadrilaterals (4-sided shapes); $\frac{6}{12} = \frac{1}{2}$
- 37 $\frac{3}{4}$ 9 out of 12 are not triangles; $\frac{9}{12} = \frac{3}{4}$
- 38 **0** No hexagons are shown.

39–42 Refer to Mixed paper 4 Q43–46 on conversion charts and read the line graph in the same way. The dotted line with circles shows 'Fiction books' and the solid line with crosses shows 'Factual books'. Between every 10 books sold, the graph has been separated into 5 equal parts, so each horizontal line represents 2 books.

- 39 **November** Only 'N' for November is level with 25 for factual books.
- 40 **April** 20 factual books and 10 fiction books were sold in April.

41 **30** Fiction books = 40; factual books = 10; 40 − 10 = 30
42 **16** November = 46; October = 30; 46 − 30 = 16
43–46 Refer to the explanation of coordinates on page 22.
43–44 **A (−4, 2), B (0, 6)**
45
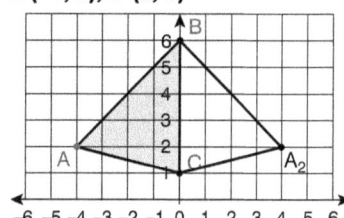
A reflection is the mirror image of a shape.
46 **(4, 2)**
47–50 **30 mm < 3.2 cm < 32 cm < 2.3 m** Change the lengths so they are all shown in the same unit of measurement. For example, change them all into cm by multiplying those shown in metres by 100 (2.3 m × 100 = 230 cm) and dividing measurements shown in mm by 10 (30 mm ÷ 10 = 3.0 cm). Then place them in order: 3.0 cm, 3.2 cm, 32 cm, 230 cm.

Mixed paper 7 (pages 51–55)

1 **37.54** As the number is between 30 and 40, the first digit must be 3; write the rest of the numbers from largest to smallest.
2–4 **6.026 < 6.062 < 6.266** < means less than, so the first number will be the smallest. Refer to Q7 on comparing decimal numbers and look for the smallest digit in each column to find the smallest number.
5–6

+	44	58
77	121	**135**
86	130	144

77 + 58 = 135; invert the other equation to subtraction (144 − 58) to find 86.
7–9 Refer to Focus test 2 Q7–12 on division.
7 **21 r 2**
8 **13 r 4**
9 **42 r 1**
10 **36 × 42** Refer to Focus test 2 Q4 on the product and long multiplication; 36 × 42 = 1512; 23 × 64 = 1472; 43 × 34 = 1462
11 **21** 1 × 21 = 21; 3 × 7 = 21, so the factors are 1, 3, 7 and 21.
12 **56** A square number is when a number is multiplied by itself (e.g. 5 × 5 = 25) so use times tables knowledge; no number can be multiplied by itself to make 56.

13 **3 × 5 × 7** Refer to the explanation of prime numbers on page 8; 3 × 5 = 15; 15 × 7 = 105
14 **7** Use times table knowledge; all the numbers shown are answers in the 7 times table; 3 × 7 = 21; 5 × 7 = 35; 12 × 7 = 84
15 **0.95** Change all the amounts into percentages and then compare (refer to the explanations of finding equivalent fractions and changing fractions into percentages on page 10); $\frac{8}{10} = \frac{80}{100} = 80\%$; $0.95 = \frac{95}{100} = 95\%$; 95% is the largest so the answer is 0.95.
16–17 A mixed number is a whole number and fraction written together (e.g. $2\frac{3}{4}$); an improper fraction is a fraction that has a numerator larger than the denominator (e.g. $\frac{11}{4}$). Change the large number into a fraction by multiplying it by the denominator (e.g. for $2\frac{3}{4}$, multiply 2 × 4 to find 8, so $2 = \frac{8}{4}$) then add the fractions ($\frac{8}{4} + \frac{3}{4} = \frac{11}{4}$).
16 $\frac{14}{5}$ 2 × 5 = 10, so $2 = \frac{10}{5}$; $\frac{10}{5} + \frac{4}{5} = \frac{14}{5}$
17 $\frac{10}{3}$ 3 × 3 = 9, so $3 = \frac{9}{3}$; $\frac{9}{3} + \frac{1}{3} = \frac{10}{3}$
18 $1\frac{1}{2}$ Refer to Focus test 5 Q1–3 on sequences; $\frac{1}{2}$ is the equivalent of $\frac{3}{6}$; write the fractions on a number line where each interval is $\frac{1}{6}$; the rule for this sequence is 'add $\frac{2}{6}$'; $1\frac{3}{6}$ is the equivalent of $1\frac{1}{2}$.

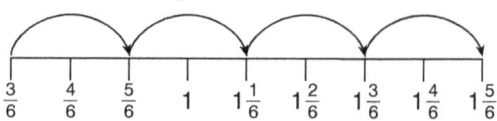

19 **100** 9 × 9 = 81, so the next square number will be the answer to 10 × 10.
20–22 Refer to Focus test 5 Q1–3 on sequences and negative numbers.
20 **1** 5 − 3 = 2; the numbers increase so the rule is 'add 2'; 2 added to −1 is 1
21 **180** The numbers increase so it is addition or multiplication; 2 × 45 = 90 and 360 × 2 = 720, so the rule is 'multiply by 2'; 2 × 90 = 180
22 **3819** 3829 − 3824 = 5; the numbers decrease so the rule is 'subtract 5'; 3824 − 5 = 3819
23–26 Refer to Focus test 6 Q1–6 on completing the inverse.
23 **11** 3s = 3 × s; 33 ÷ 3 = 11
24 **6** 2d = 18 (2 × 9) and 3f = 12 (3 × 4); 18 − 12 = 6
25 **19** 61 − 42 = 19
26 **3** $\frac{24}{g} = 24 \div g$; 24 ÷ 8 = 3

27 **parallelogram**

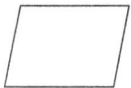

28 **50°** Refer to Focus test 7 Q12 on using a protractor.
29 **obtuse** Obtuse angles are between 90° and 180°.
30 **scalene** A scalene triangle has sides that are all different lengths.
31–34 Refer to the explanations of area and perimeter on pages 18–19, Focus test 6 Q10 on adding decimal numbers and Focus test 8 Q5 on multiplying decimal numbers.
31 **15 m** 3.5 + 4.0 = 7.5; 7.5 × 2 = 15
32 **12.4 m** 5.0 + 1.2 = 6.2; 6.2 × 2 = 12.4
33 **A** Shape A = 3.5 × 4 =14; shape B = 5 × 1.2 = 6; 10 > 6
34 **12 cm** As the shape is a square, all sides are the same length; 3 × 3 = 9, so each side is 3 cm; 3 + 3 = 6; 6 × 2 = 12
35 **12 cm** Multiply 1.7 m by 100 to change it into cm (refer to Focus test 1 Q5 on multiplying by 100); 1.7 m = 170 cm; 170 − 158 = 12
36 **14°C** Between every 10°C the scales have been separated into 10 equal parts, so each of the smallest lines represents 1°C (10 ÷ 10 = 1); the first thermometer shows 7°C and the second shows −7°C; the difference between −7 and 7 is 14 (refer to Focus test 6 Q3 on negative numbers).
37 **45 minutes** Refer to Mixed paper 2 Q37 on calculating elapsed time; 9:50 to 10:00 = 10 mins; 10:00 to 10:35 = 35 mins; 10 + 35 = 45
38 **2750 ml** Between each litre, the jug has been separated into 4 equal parts; 1 litre = 1000 ml and 1000 ÷ 4 = 250 ml, so each small line represents 250 ml; the grey shaded area is level with the third line after 2 litres (2000 ml); 3 × 250 = 750; 2000 + 750 = 2750
39–42 Refer to the explanation of coordinates and translation on pages 22–23.
39 **(−1, 2)**
40–41 Point B has moved from (1, 2) to (−3, 1) so the shape has moved **4** squares to the left (**4** subtracted from 1 = −3) and **1** down (**1** subtracted from 2 = 1), so all the other points will move in the same way.
42 **(−5, 1) 4** subtracted from −1 = −5; **1** subtracted from 2 = 1
43–46 Refer to the explanation of reading graphs on page 25; between every £1.00, the chart has been separated into 10 equal parts, so each vertical line represents £0.10 (or 10p) and halfway between them represents £0.05 (or 5p). Look to see which numbers the grey bars are level with.

43 **Anu** The bars are only equal height for Anu.
44 **Matt** Jia saved £1.00 and spent £3.00 and £1.00 + £3.00 = £4.00 in total; Matt saved £1.75 and spent £2.25; £1.75 + £2.25 = £4.00 in total
45 **Haseeb** There is no light grey bar shown for Haseeb.
46 **Kim** Add the numbers the light and dark grey bars are level with for each child; £2.00 + £2.50 = £4.50
47–50 Refer to the explanation of mean, median, mode and range on page 26.
47 **40** 35 + 40 + 35 + 45 + 35 + 40 + 50 = 280; 280 ÷ 7 = 40
48 **40** 35, 35, 35, 40, 40, 45, 50; the number in the middle is 40.
49 **35** 35 occurs the most often.
50 **15** 50 − 35 = 15

Mixed paper 8 (pages 56–60)

1–3 Refer to Focus test 1 Q5 on multiplying and dividing by 10, 100 and 1000
1 **1000**
2 **100**
3 **10**
4 **0.26** Refer to Focus test 1 Q4 on rounding. As the number rounds to 0.3, it will be between 0.25 and 0.34; only 0.26 has 2 digits that add up to 8.
5 **78** Partition 14 into 10 and 4 (as 10 + 4 = 14), then subtract each number in turn; 92 − 10 = 82; 82 − 4 = 78
6 **180** Partition 42 into 40 and 2 (as 40 + 2 = 42), then add each number in turn; 138 + 40 = 178; 178 + 2 = 180
7–12 Refer to Focus test 2 Q4 on long multiplication.
7 **1168** 8 **975** 9 **1944**
10 **450 ÷ 8** Refer to Focus test 2 Q7–12 on division; 378 ÷ 7 = 54; 615 ÷ 9 = 68 r 3; 450 ÷ 8 = 56 **r 2**; 381 ÷ 4 = 95 r 1
11–12 **3 and 14** Refer to the explanation of factors on page 8; 3 × 14 = 42 and 3 + 14 = 17
13–14 Refer to the explanation of multiples on page 9; multiply the numbers together (the multiple will not be higher than the answer), then find the lowest number in both groups.
13 **36** 9 × 4 = 36
14 **24** 3 × 8 = 24 and 4 × 6 = 24

15–18

Fraction	$\frac{3}{10}$	$\frac{7}{100}$	$\frac{2}{5}$	$\frac{4}{5}$
Decimal	0.3	0.07	0.4	0.8
Percentage	30%	7%	40%	80%

Refer to the explanations of equivalent fractions, changing fractions into percentages and percentages into fractions on page 10 and

Focus test 4 Q1–4 on simplifying; $\frac{7}{100}$ = 7%; $\frac{2}{5} = \frac{40}{100}$ = 0.40; 80% = $\frac{80}{100}$ = 0.80; $\frac{80}{100}$ can be simplified to $\frac{4}{5}$.

19–22 Refer to Focus test 5 Q1–3 on sequences and subtracting decimal numbers and Focus test 6 Q10 on adding decimal numbers.

19 **7.5** 3.0 − 1.5 = 1.5; the numbers increase so the rule is 'add 1.5'; 6.0 + 1.5 = 7.5.

20 **$2\frac{1}{4}$** Write the fractions on a number line where the difference between each fraction is $\frac{1}{4}$; the rule is 'add $\frac{2}{4}$' $1\frac{3}{4} + \frac{2}{4} = 2\frac{1}{4}$

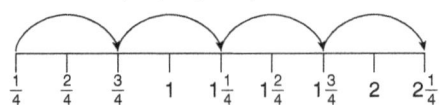

21 **1.5** 0.9 − 0.7 = 0.2; the numbers increase so the rule is 'add 0.2'; 1.3 + 0.2 = 1.5.

22 **0.5** 10.5 − 8.0 = 2.5; the numbers decrease so the rule is 'subtract 2.5'; 3.0 − 2.5 = 0.5.

23–24 Count the squares shown on the grid.

Ring (r)	1	2	3	4	5
Squares (s)	8	16	24	32	40

25 **8r = s** The number of rings has been multiplied by 8 each time; 8 × r is the same as 8r.

26 **80** 10 rings × 8 = 80 squares

27 **square-based pyramid**

28 **5 vertices** A vertex is a corner where 3 or more faces and edges meet.

29 **sometimes** Although 2 sides on an isosceles triangle are always the same size and length, the third angle can be any angle up to 180°, including a right angle, as shown.

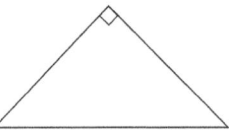

30 **75°** Angles in a triangle always add up to 180°; 180 − 30 = 150, so x + x = 150; divide by 2 to find x; 150 ÷ 2 = 75

31–34 Refer to the explanations of area and perimeter on pages 18–19.

31 **500 m²** 2 × 25 = 50 so 20 × 25 = 500

32 **3000 m²** Find the area of the garden, then subtract the area of the house; 7 × 5 = 35, so 70 × 50 = 3500; 3500 − 500 = 3000

33 **90 m** 25 + 20 = 45; 45 × 2 = 90

34 **240 m** 70 + 50 = 120; 120 × 2 = 240

35 **650 ml** Refer to Focus test 9 Q9 on reading scales. The first jug shows 600 ml and the second jug shows $1\frac{1}{4}$ litres; $1\frac{1}{4}$ litres = 1250 ml and 1250 − 600 = 650.

36 **1.85 litres** 1250 + 600 = 1850; 1 litre = 1000 ml, so divide by 1000; 1850 ÷ 1000 = 1.850 which is the same as 1.85.

37 **<** < means less than and > means greater than; 1 kg = 1000 g, so multiply by 1000; 3.5 × 1000 = 3500; 350 < 3500

38 **10** 1 m = 100 cm, so 3 m = 300 cm; 300 ÷ 30 = 10

39–41 Refer to the explanation of coordinates on page 22.

39 **A (−4, −1)**

40 **C (0, 2)**

41 **T (6, −1)**

42 **reflection** Refer to the explanation of transformations on page 23; the letters shown refer to the corners of each parallelogram.

43–46 Refer to Mixed paper 4 Q43–46 on conversion charts and read the graph in the same way. Between every 5 km, the chart has been separated into 5 equal parts, so each vertical line represents 1 km.

43 **3 km** The part of the line 2:00 crosses is level with 3 km.

44 **2 km** 2:00 = 3 km and 2:30 = 5 km; 5 − 3 = 2

45 **3:00–3:30 p.m.** The lines stays at 7 km between 3:00 and 3:30.

46 **4:15 p.m.** The line is level with halfway between 4:00 and 4:30; 4:00 to 4:30 = 30 mins, so divide by 2 to find halfway; 30 ÷ 2 = 15, so the time is 4:15.

47–50 As there are 12 cards, write the fraction with a denominator of 12 to begin with, then simplify (refer to Focus test 4 Q1–4 on simplifying fractions).

47 **$\frac{1}{2}$** 6 out of 12 are even numbers; $\frac{6}{12} = \frac{1}{2}$

48 **$\frac{1}{4}$** 3 out of 12 are multiples of 4 (the numbers 4, 8 and 12); $\frac{3}{12} = \frac{1}{4}$

49 **$\frac{3}{4}$** 9 out of 12 numbers have 1 digit; $\frac{9}{12} = \frac{3}{4}$

50 **0** The number 13 is not shown, so it is 'impossible'.

NOTES

NOTES

39 Write the coordinates of point A. (__, __)

40 Plot C at (2, 6) and draw lines from B to C and A to C to complete the triangle.

41 Circle the coordinates that will be inside this triangle.

(4, 2)   (2, 1)   (3, 2)

(1, 4)   (2, 3)   (1, 2)

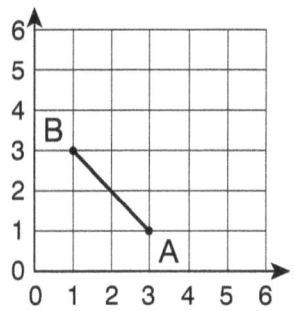

42 Translate this triangle 3 squares to the right. Draw the triangle in the new position.

The children in a school measured their heights to the nearest centimetre. This chart shows the range of their heights.

43 What range of height were most children? _____

44 How many children were over 150 cm high? _____

45 How many more children were between 131–140 cm than were 130 cm or under? _____

46 Underline the correct height group for a child that is 160 cm tall.

151–160 cm   over 160 cm

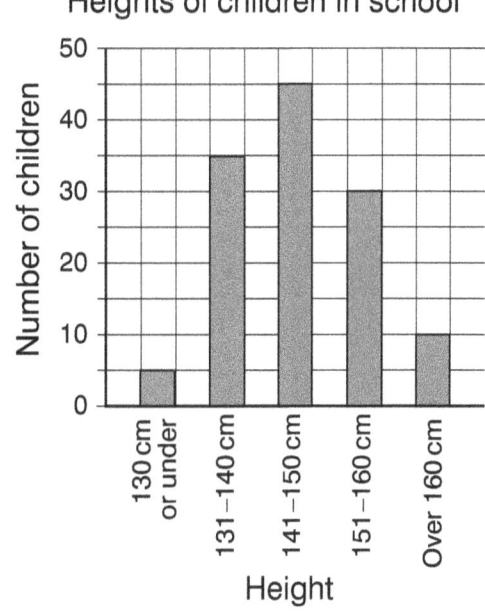

Heights of children in school

47 What coin value is the mode? _____

48 What is the mean value of the coins? _____

49 Which coin value is the median? _____

50 What is the range? _____

Now go to the Progress Chart to record your score!   Total   50

Mixed paper 2

Round each distance to the nearest whole metre.

1 839.5 m _____   2 107.48 m _____

Complete these calculations.

3 826 ÷ 100 = _____   4 1095 ÷ 100 = _____

Complete these calculations.

5
```
   52.6
 -  8.5
 _____
```

6
```
   75.3
 - 14.9
 _____
```

7 20 × 400 = _____   8 8 × 21 = _____

9 196 ÷ 7 = _____   10 258 ÷ 6 = _____

11–12 Circle the numbers that are multiples of 8.

62   96   78   46   24   30

Is each statement true or false? Circle the answer.

13 17 is a factor of 68.   True / False

14 74 is a multiple of 6.   True / False

Write <, > or = to make each statement true.

15 $\frac{4}{5}$ ___ $\frac{9}{10}$ 16 $\frac{3}{4}$ ___ $\frac{2}{3}$

17 Gina has collected 1p and 2p coins. There are 30 coins in total and $\frac{2}{3}$ are 1p coins. How many 1p coins does Gina have? _____

18 Jake mixes 1 spoon of fruit with every 5 spoons of yoghurt. For breakfast he has 3 spoons of fruit. How many spoons of yoghurt does he have? _____

Write the missing numbers in these sequences.

19–20 _____ 8   16   32   64   _____

21–22 _____   358   408   458   508   _____

Write the missing numbers in these equations.

23 23 + _____ = 31

24 _____ ÷ 4 = 9

25 _____ − 25 = 32

26 5 × _____ = 45

Write the number of faces, edges and vertices on a tetrahedron.

27–29 Faces = _____   Edges = _____   Vertices = _____

30 Use a protractor to measure this angle. Angle x = _____ °

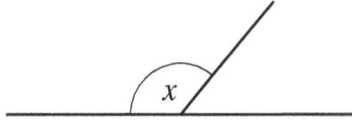

Calculate the area and perimeter of each of these.

5 cm
14 cm

9 cm

31 Area = _____ cm²

32 Perimeter = _____ cm

33 Area = _____ cm²

34 Perimeter = _____ cm

Write the temperature shown on each thermometer.

35

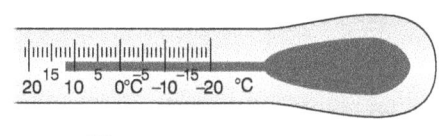

_____ °C

36

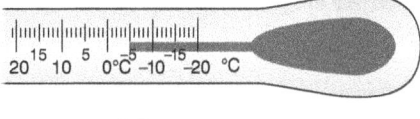

_____ °C

37 A film starts at 19:30 and ends at 21:05. How long does the film last?
_____ h _____ min

38 What is 3.7 kg in grams? _____ g

39–41 Draw another triangle at the following coordinates: (4, 2) (6, 4) (8, 0). Label it B.

42 Is triangle B a **translation**, **rotation** or **reflection** of triangle A? _____

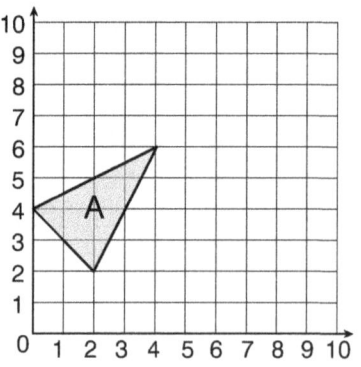

This pie chart shows the result of a traffic survey. There was a total of 200 vehicles in the survey.

43 What fraction of the traffic were vans? _____

44 What percentage of the traffic were bicycles?

_____

45 How many cars were there? _____

46 How many more vans than lorries were there?

_____

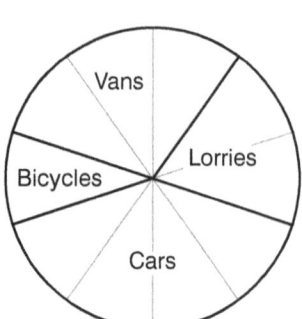

Underline the chance for each of these.

47 What is the chance you will see a hot air balloon today?

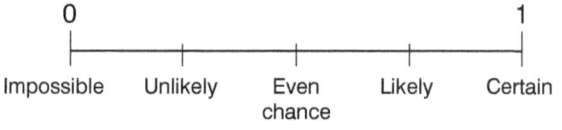

48 What is the chance the sun will shine at midnight?

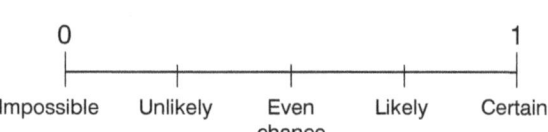

49 What is the chance that you will blink today?

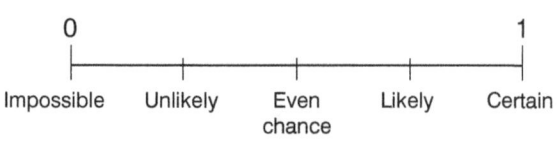

50 What is the chance you will go to bed before midnight?

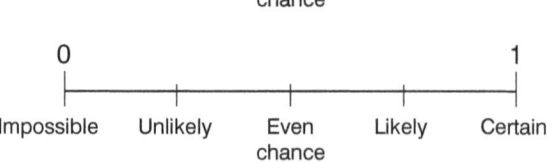

Mixed paper 3

1. A plum weighs 58 g. Would you estimate the weight of other plums to the nearest **10 g**, **100 g** or **1000 g**? _____

2–3. Circle the smallest number and underline the largest number.

23.9   9.392   23.09   9.93   29.3   9.299

4. What is £146.55 to the nearest whole pound? £_____

Write <, > or = to make each statement true.

5. 54 + 17 ___ 123 − 51

6. 140 − 84 ___ 27 + 33

7–10. This is a 'divide by 30' machine. Write the missing numbers in the chart.

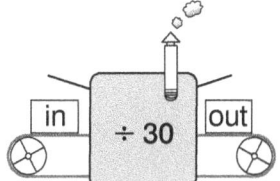

IN	270		300		600
OUT	9	5		8	

11–12. Which two factors of 36 are missing from this list? _____ and _____

1   2   3   6   12   18   36

13. What is the next prime number after 23? _____

14. $10^2 \div \sqrt{25}$ = _____

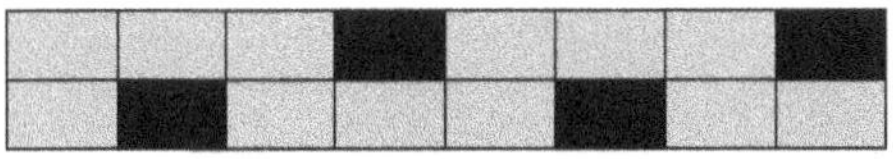

15. What is the ratio of black tiles to grey tiles? _____

16–17. This tile pattern is used on a floor that will need 80 tiles in total. How many of each colour tile will be needed?

Black → _____ tiles   Grey → _____ tiles

18. Circle the fraction that is equivalent to $\frac{1}{3}$

$\frac{3}{4}$ $\frac{5}{9}$ $\frac{3}{10}$ $\frac{5}{15}$ $\frac{4}{6}$ $\frac{3}{15}$

19. $3^2 + 5^2$ = _____

Write the missing number in each sequence

20 12   20   ____   36   44

21 145   142   ____   136   133

22 150   300   ____   600   750

Calculate these, when $r = 5$.

23 $23 + r =$ ____

24 $4r =$ ____

What number does each letter represent?

25 $34 - a = 25$ $a =$ ____

26 $6b = 18$ $b =$ ____

Look at this pentagon.

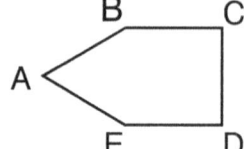

27 Which line is parallel to line BC? Line ____

28 Which line is perpendicular to line ED? Line ____

29 Describe the angle at A. Circle the correct answer.

   right   acute   obtuse   reflex

30 Draw a line of symmetry on the pentagon.

What is the area and perimeter of this square?

11 cm

31 Area = ____ cm²

32 Perimeter = ____ cm

33 Draw a square with an area of 25 cm². Use a ruler.

34 What is the perimeter of the square you have drawn? ____ cm

35 How much water is in this jug? _____ litres

36 400 ml of the water in this jug is poured into a glass. How much water will be left in the jug?

_____ ml

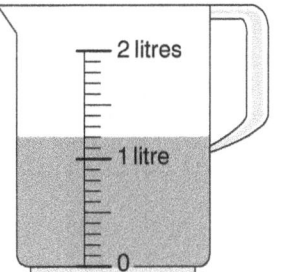

Look at this clock.

This is the time a bus leaves the bus station in the morning. The journey to a school is 25 minutes long.

37 What time will the bus arrive at the school? _____

38 In the afternoon the bus arrives at the school at 3:20 p.m. What time did the bus leave the bus station? _____

Look at the quadrilaterals A, B and C. Complete these sentences with **translation**, **rotation** or **reflection**.

39 Shape C is a _____ of shape A.

40 Shape B is a _____ of shape C.

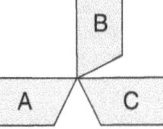

41–42 Circle the coordinates of A and underline the coordinates of B.

(3, −4)   (3, 4)   (4, −3)

(−4, 3)   (4, 3)

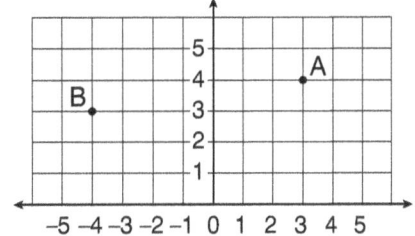

The numbers 1–40 have been sorted on this Venn diagram.

43–44 The last two numbers are missing. Write **39** and **40** in the correct place on the Venn diagram.

45 Which number is a **square number**, an **even number** and a **multiple of 3**? _____

46 How many **multiples of 3** are there in total between 1 and 40? _____

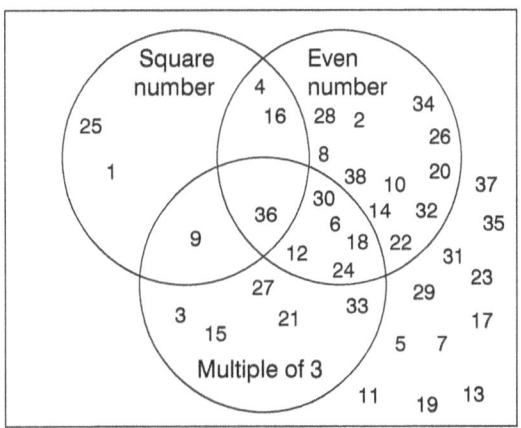

These are Red group's spelling test scores.

Michel	Tanya	Will	Piotr	Fay
17	18	15	20	15

47 What is the mean score? _____

48 What is the median score? _____

49 What is the mode? _____

50 What is the range? _____

Now go to the Progress Chart to record your score! Total 50

Mixed paper 4

Read this number word and write all your answers using digits.

| seven hundred and fifty-two thousand nine hundred and six |

1 Write the number that is 100 more. _____

2 What number is 1000 less? _____

3 Round the number word to the nearest 1000. _____

4 Write the number that is 1000 more than the number word. _____

Mr Day bought two chairs for £39.49 each and a table for £114.99.

5 How much did he spend in total? £_____

6 How much change did he get from £200? £_____

7 Use this grid to help you multiply 237 by 30.

×	200	30	7
30				→ _____

8 $\quad$ 347 × 8

9 $\quad$ 208 × 9

10 Divide 99 by 7. _____

Write <, > or = to make each statement true.

11 3^2 _____ $\sqrt{81}$

12 $\sqrt{144}$ _____ 4^2

13–14 Circle the two prime numbers in this set.

51   37   49   29   35   27

There are 12 fish in a tank. 6 are orange, 4 are green and 2 are blue.

15 Circle the proportion of the fish that are green.

$\frac{1}{2}$ $\frac{1}{3}$ $\frac{1}{4}$ $\frac{1}{6}$

16 What percentage of the fish are orange? _____

17–18 Circle the two cards that show less than $\frac{1}{2}$.

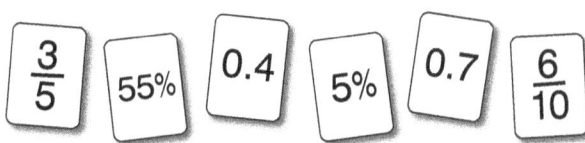

Write the next two numbers in each sequence.

19–20 49   36   25   16   _____   _____

21–22 489   487   485   483   _____   _____

Write the value of each letter in these equations.

23 $16 + m = 70$ $m =$ _____   **24** $3n = 27$ $n =$ _____

A recipe makes 10 biscuits using 6 cups of flour and 2 eggs.

25–26 How many cups of flour and eggs will be needed to make 30 biscuits?

_____ cups of flour   _____ eggs

27–30 Write the letter for each shape in the correct section on this chart.

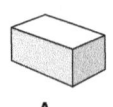 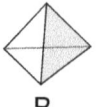 

A   B   C   D

	Pyramid	Prism
Shape letter		

Calculate the area and perimeter of each of these.

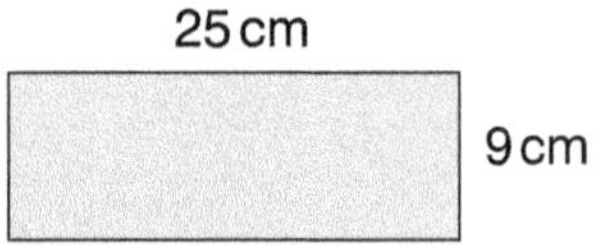

25 cm   9 cm   12 cm

31 Area = _____ cm²

32 Perimeter = _____ cm

33 Area = _____ cm²

34 Perimeter = _____ cm

Complete these conversions.

35 670 mm = _____ cm

36 0.9 l = _____ ml

37 8.4 m = _____ cm

38 3800 g = _____ kg

39 Write the coordinates of point C.

(___, ___)

40 Line AB and line BC are two sides of a rectangle. Plot the missing fourth vertex and label it D. Draw lines to complete the rectangle.

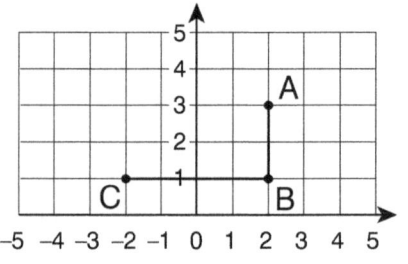

41 Write the coordinates of point D. (___, ___)

42 Circle the flag that is a rotation of the first flag.

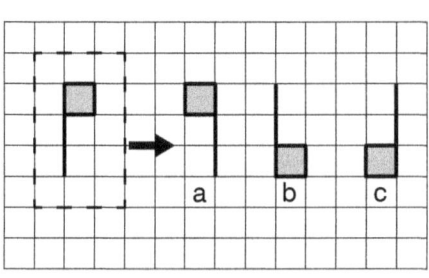

a   b   c

This is a conversion chart for changing kilograms to pounds, and pounds to kilograms.

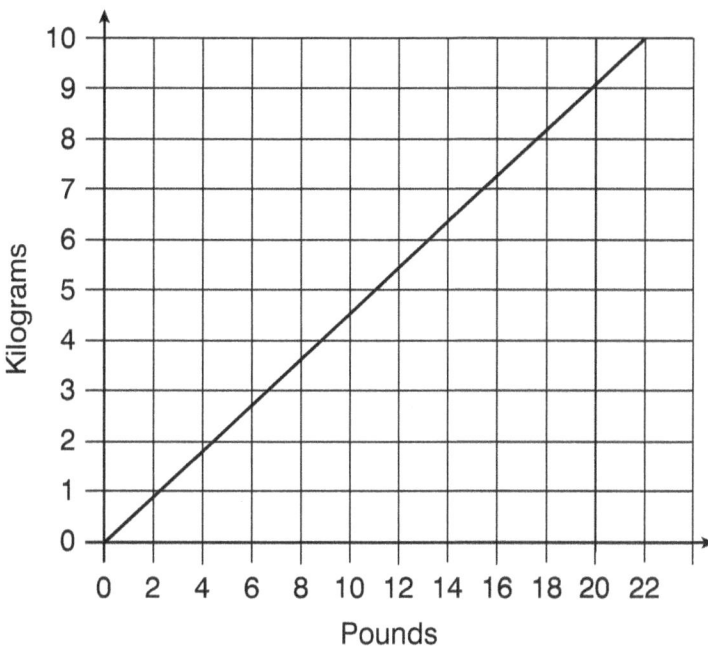

43 How many pounds are approximately the same as 10 kilograms? _____ lb

44 How many kilograms are approximately the same as 11 pounds? _____ kg

45 An old recipe uses 2 pounds of flour in a loaf of bread. Approximately how much flour would be the same in kilograms? Round your answer to the nearest whole kilogram. ___ kg

46 Which is heavier, 6 kilograms or 6 pounds? _____

Underline the chance of rolling each of these on fair dice.
What is the chance of rolling:

47 An odd number?

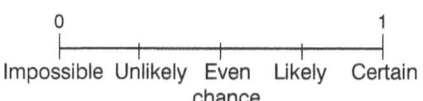

49 A multiple of 3?

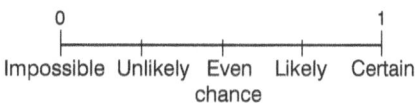

48 The number 1?

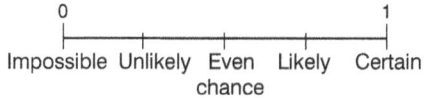

50 The number 7?

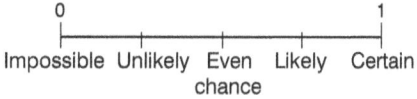

Now go to the Progress Chart to record your score!   Total   50

Mixed paper 5

Round each amount to the nearest tenth.

1 26.507 rounds to _____

2 349.061 rounds to _____

3–4 Write the numbers at each arrow.

5 What is 5406 more than 1946? _____

6 What is 3778 less than 7200? _____

7 Use this grid to multiply 78 by 23.

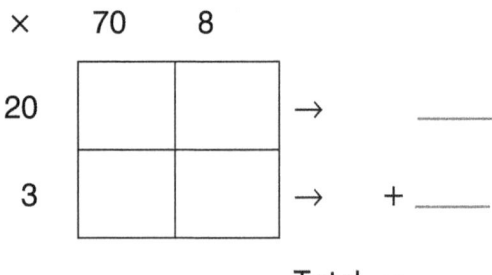

8 Eggs are sold in boxes of 12. How many full boxes can be filled from 70 eggs? _____

9 A car needs 4 new tyres. One tyre costs £60. How much will it cost to replace all 4 tyres? £_____

10 There are 32 children in a class. Exercise books are sold in packs of 8. How many packs will be needed for each child to have 3 books? _____

11 What is the common factor of 12 and 27? _____

Complete these sentences with **always**, **sometimes** or **never**.

12 A prime number will _____ have an even number of factors.

13 A square number will _____ have an even number of factors.

14 What is the largest factor of 18, not including 18 itself? ____

Look at this rectangle.

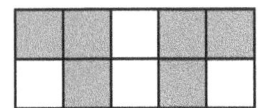

15 What fraction of this rectangle is shaded? Write the fraction in its lowest terms. ___

16 What percentage of this rectangle is white? ____%

Write < or > to make each statement true.

17 0.64 ___ 0.46

18 0.07 ___ 0.7

Write the next number in each sequence.

19   4.5   5   5.5   6   ____

20   $1\frac{1}{4}$ $1\frac{1}{2}$ $1\frac{3}{4}$ 2   ____

21   12   9   6   3   ____

22   10   0   −10   −20   ____

Calculate these, when $h = 7$ and $k = 8$.

23   $5h - 3k =$ ____

24   $3h + 2k =$ ____

What number does each letter represent?

25   $56 - a = 29$ $a =$ ____

26   $9b = 81$ $b =$ ____

27 This quadrilateral has no parallel sides.

True or False? _____

28 Calculate the size of angle *d*. Angle *d* = ___°

29 Circle the name of this quadrilateral.

    trapezium   kite   parallelogram   rectangle

30 I am a shape with 5 faces, 5 vertices and 8 edges. How many of my faces are triangles? _____

Calculate the area of each rectangle.

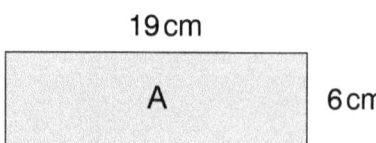
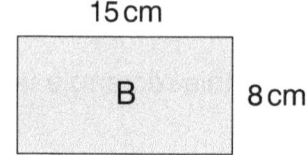

31 Area of A = _____ cm²

32 Area of B = _____ cm²

33 Which shape has the longer perimeter, A or B? _____

34 Draw a rectangle on the grid with a perimeter of 18 cm and an area of 18 square centimetres. Use a ruler.

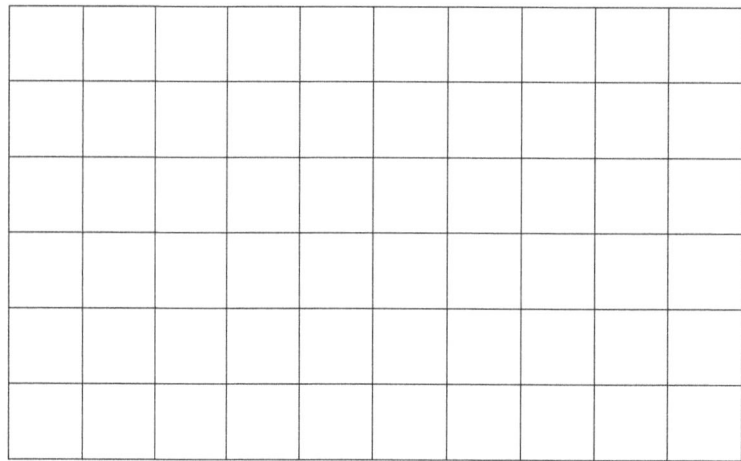

35 A carton of fruit juice fills 5 glasses each holding 400 ml of juice. How much juice was in the carton? Circle the correct answer.

    1 litre   1.6 litres   2 litres   2.5 litres

36 A man is 6 feet tall. Approximately how many metres tall is this man?
   _____ m

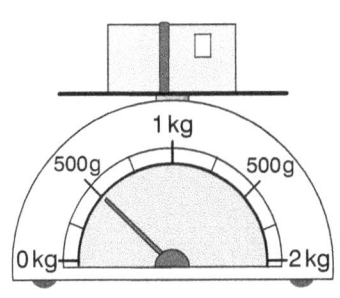 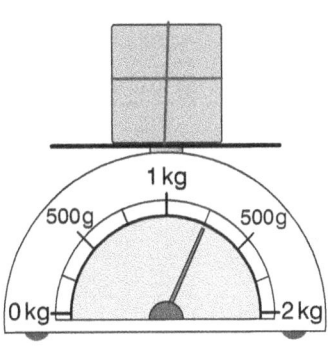

37 What is the difference in weight between these two parcels, in grams?
   _____ g
38 What is the total weight of these two parcels, in kilograms? _____ kg

Write **translation**, **rotation** or **reflection** to identify how each pattern was made with the L-shaped tiles.

39   40   41

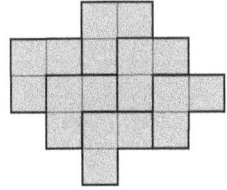   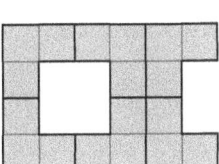   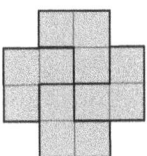

_____   _____   _____

42 Point A is at (−3, 0). Plot this point and label it.

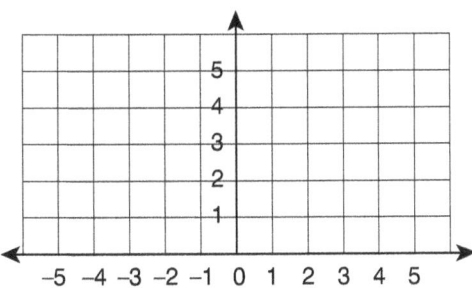

This block graph shows the amount of water a family uses in 1 week.

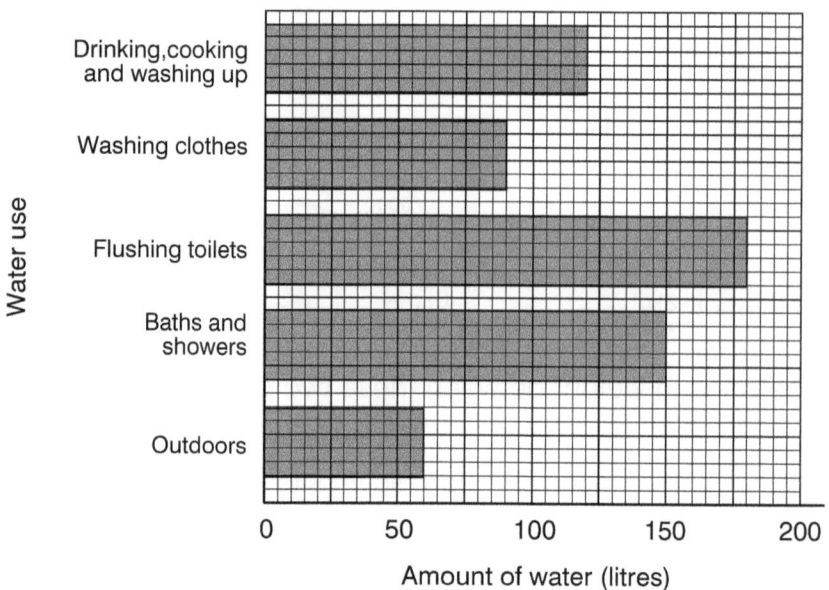

43 Which activity uses 90 litres of water? _____

44 How many litres of water are used outdoors? _____ litres

45 How much more water is used drinking, cooking and washing up, than washing clothes? _____ litres

46 How many litres of water in total are used flushing toilets and for baths and showers? _____ litres

These are the weights of nine oranges.

    55 g   40 g   45 g   55 g   80 g   40 g   55 g   40 g   40 g

47 What is the mean? _____

48 What is the median? _____

49 What is the mode? _____

50 What is the range? _____

Now go to the Progress Chart to record your score!   Total

Mixed paper 6

1–4 Change each of these lengths from metres into centimetres and millimetres.

Metres	Centimetres	Millimetres
6.4 m	_____ cm	_____ mm
5.01 m	_____ cm	_____ mm

5–6 Write the missing digits in this addition.

```
   □ 8 1
 + 2 □ 9
 ─────────
   8 6 0
```

Write <, > or = to make each statement true.

7 19 × 6 ___ 3 × 38

8 72 ÷ 4 ___ 57 ÷ 3

Solve these and write your answers as numbers not words.

9 Divide five hundred and forty-six by seven. _____

10 Share seven hundred and sixty-eight by eight. _____

11–13 What are the common factors of 28 and 70?

1, _____, _____ and _____

14 Which prime number is closest to 4^2? _____

15 What is $\frac{3}{4}$ of 20? _____

Complete these equivalent fractions.

16 $\frac{1}{2} = \frac{10}{\square}$

17 $\frac{4}{5} = \frac{\square}{10}$

18 There are 50 eggs in a tray and 10 are broken. What percentage of the eggs are broken? _____ %

Write the two missing numbers in each sequence.

19–20 _____   4730   4745   4760   _____

21–22 _____   0.4   0.6   0.8   _____

Write the value of each of these letters.

23 $4q - 10 = 10$ $q =$ _____

24 $3p + 4 = 10$ $p =$ _____

What number does y represent in each equation?

25 $3y - 2 = 4$ $y =$ _____

26 $2y + 1 = 9$ $y =$ _____

Write the size of the missing angle in each of these triangles.

27

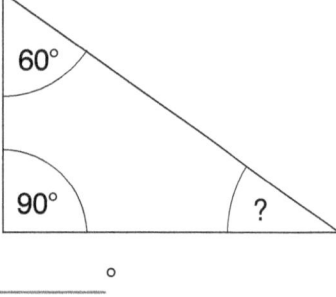

_____ °

28

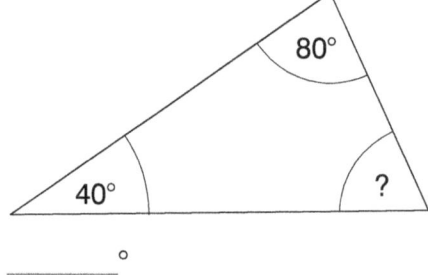

_____ °

29–30 How many rectangles and how many triangles are there on the net of a triangular prism?

_____ rectangles   _____ triangles

31 A volleyball court is 18 m long by 9 m wide. There is a white line all the way round the court. How long is the white line? _____

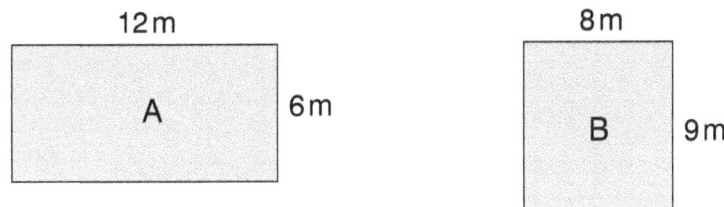

32 Underline the statement that is true.

A has a greater area than B.   B has a greater area than A.

A and B have the same area.

33 What is the difference in length between the perimeters of rectangles A and B? _____

34 What is the area of a rectangular pond that is 2.5 m by 3 m? _____ m²

All these shapes are placed in a bag and one shape is picked out at random each time and then replaced.

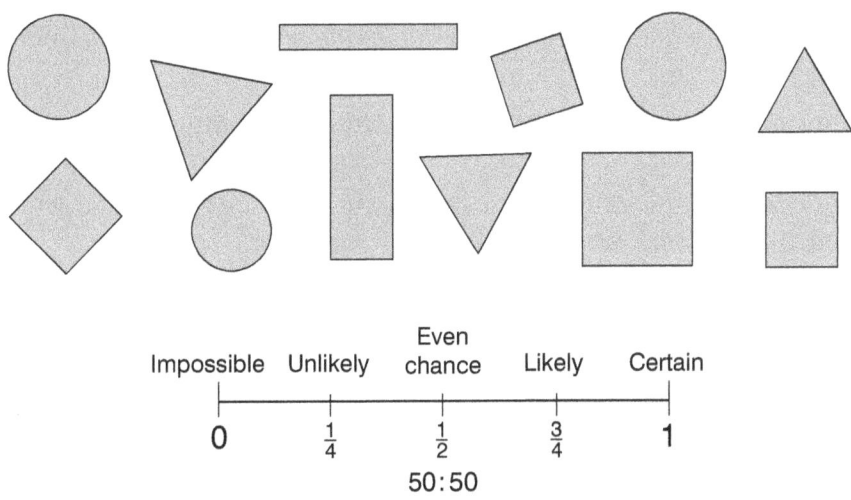

What is the likelihood of picking these? Look at the probability scale and write each answer as a fraction in its lowest terms.

35 What is the likelihood of picking a circle? ___

36 What is the likelihood of picking a quadrilateral? ___

37 What is the likelihood of **not** picking a triangle? ___

38 Circle the likelihood of picking a hexagon.

0   50:50   1

This graph shows the monthly sales of factual and fiction books in a bookshop.

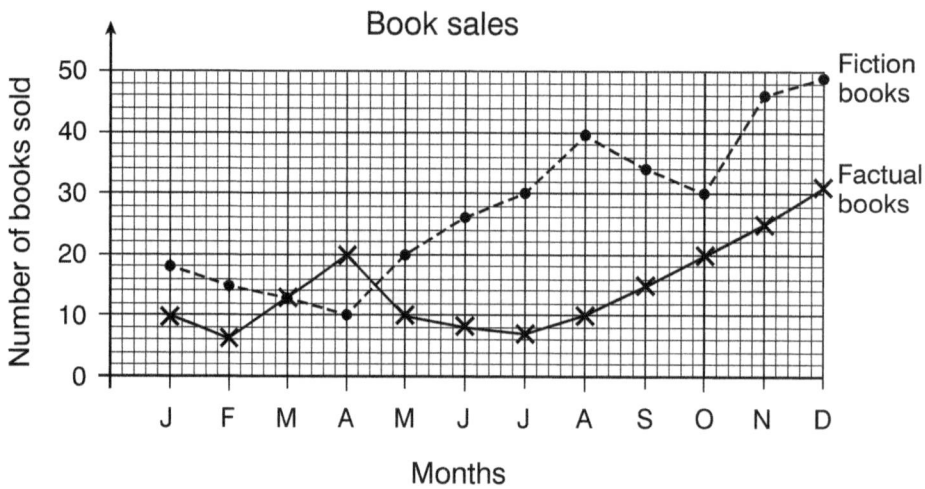

39 In which month were 25 factual books sold? _____

40 In which month were more factual books than fiction books sold? _____

41 How many more fiction books than factual books were sold in August? ___

42 How many more fiction books were sold in November than in October? ___

43–44 Write the coordinates of A and B.

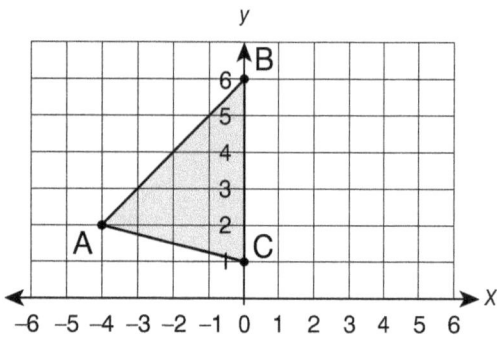

A → (___, ___)   B → (___, ___)

45 Draw the reflection of triangle ABC using the y-axis as the mirror line. Use the letter A_2 to label the reflection of point A.

46 Circle the correct coordinates of A_2.

(2, 4)   (4, 2)   (−2, 4)   (2, −4)

47–50 Write this set of measurements in length order, starting with the shortest.

3.2 cm   30 mm   2.3 m   32 cm

_____ < _____ < _____ < _____

Now go to the Progress Chart to record your score!   Total

Mixed paper 7

1 Use these four digits and the decimal point to make the largest possible decimal number between 30 and 40.

__ __ . __ __

2–4 Write these in order, starting with the smallest.

6.062   6.266   6.026

_____ < _____ < _____

5–6 Write the missing numbers on this addition grid.

+	44	58
77	121	
	130	144

Complete these calculations.

7 8)170 = __ r __

8 9)121 = __ r __

9 7)295 = __ r __

10 Circle the multiplication that has the largest product.

36 × 42   23 × 64   43 × 34

11 Which of these numbers has four factors?

21   23   24   25   28

12 Circle the number that is **not** a square number in this set.

36   64   16   9   56   25

13 Which three consecutive **prime** numbers multiply to make 105?

____ × ____ × ____ = 105

14 Apart from 1, what is the common factor of 21, 35 and 84? ____

15 Which is the largest: $\frac{8}{10}$, **0.95** or **85%**? ____

Circle the improper fraction with the same value as the mixed number.

16 $2\frac{4}{5}$ $\frac{24}{5}$ $\frac{8}{5}$ $\frac{14}{5}$ $\frac{10}{5}$

17 $3\frac{1}{3}$ $\frac{13}{3}$ $\frac{10}{3}$ $\frac{9}{3}$ $\frac{4}{3}$

18 Write the missing fraction in this sequence.

$\frac{1}{2}$ $\frac{5}{6}$ $1\frac{1}{6}$ ____ $1\frac{5}{6}$

19 What is the next square number after 81? ____

Write the missing number in each sequence.

20 −3   −1   ____   3   5

21 45   90   ____   360   720

22 3829   3824   ____   3814   3809

23 What is the value of s?

$3s = 33$ $s =$ _____

24 Complete this, when $d = 9$ and $f = 4$.

$2d - 3f =$ _____

Write the value for each of these.

25 $61 - \nabla = 42$ $\nabla =$ _____   **26** $\frac{24}{g} = 8$ $g =$ _____

27 A shape has four sides. Each pair of opposite sides are parallel and the same length. The shape has no right angles and no lines of symmetry. Opposite angles are the same size. Circle the correct name for this shape.

trapezium   rectangle   parallelogram   kite   square

Look at this triangle.

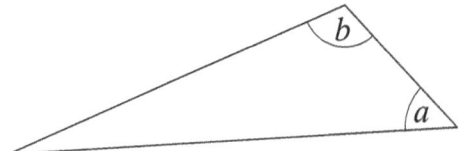

28 Use a protractor to measure the size of angle a. Angle $a =$ _____ °

29 Circle the name of angle b.

right   obtuse   reflex   acute

30 Circle the name of this type of triangle.

scalene   equilateral   isosceles   right-angled

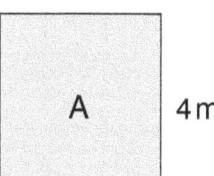

31 What is the perimeter of rectangle A? _____ m

32 What is the perimeter of rectangle B? _____ m

33 Which rectangle has the greater area, A or B? _____

34 What is the perimeter of a square with an area of 9 cm²? _____ cm

35 John is 158 cm tall and his dad is 1.7 m tall. How much shorter is John than his dad? _____ cm

36 What is the difference in temperature between these two thermometers? _____ °C

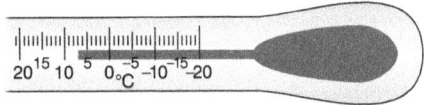 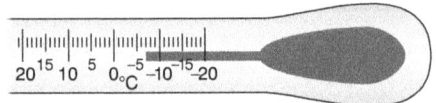

37 A maths lesson starts at 9:50am and finishes at 10:35am. How long is this maths lesson? _____

38 How much water is in this jug? Write your answer in millilitres. _____ ml

39 Circle the correct coordinates for point A.

(2, −1)   (−1, −2)   (−2, −1)

(−1, 2)   (−1, 0)

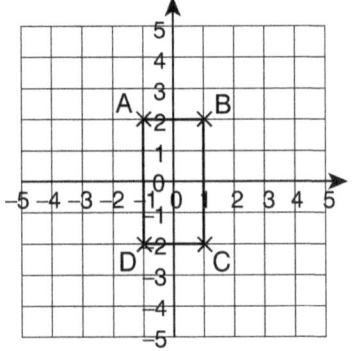

40–41 The shape is translated. Point B moves to (−3, 1) and point D moves to (−5, −3). Plot these two points and label them B_2 and D_2.

42 Where will point A_2 be on the translated shape? (_____, _____)

This graph shows how much pocket money each child gets and how they use their pocket money.

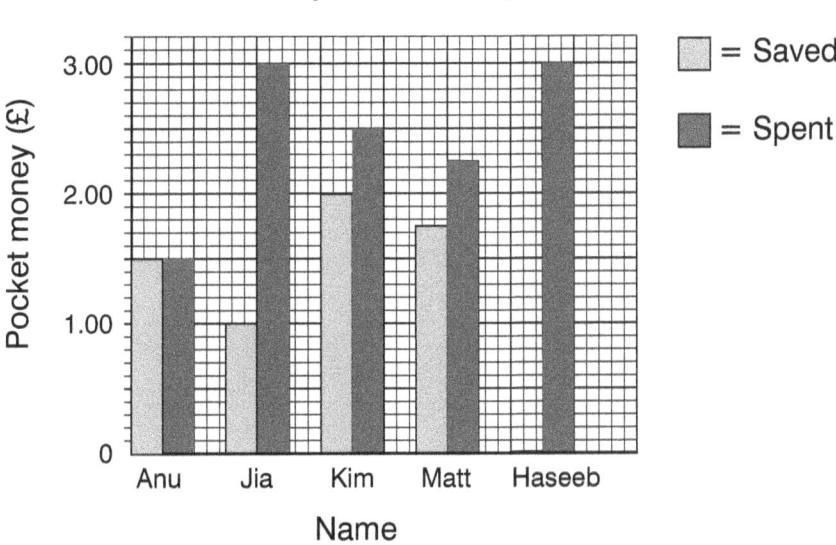

43 Who saved the same amount of money as they spent? _____

44 Who got the same amount of pocket money in total as Jon?
_____

45 Who did not save any money? _____

46 Who got the most pocket money in total? _____

These are the number of pages in each chapter of a book.

Chapter	1	2	3	4	5	6	7
Pages	35	40	35	45	35	40	50

47 What is the mean number of pages in each chapter? _____

48 What is the median number of pages in each chapter? _____

49 What is the mode? _____

50 What is the range? _____

Now go to the Progress Chart to record your score!   Total   50

Mixed paper 8

Write the missing numbers in these. Choose from **10**, **100** or **1000**.

1. 37.05 × _____ = 37 050
2. 940.7 ÷ _____ = 9.407
3. 8.118 × _____ = 81.18

4. I am thinking of a number less than 1. The two digits total 8 and the number rounds to 0.3 to the nearest tenth.

   What number am I thinking of? _____

Calculate these.

5. 92 − 14 = _____
6. 42 + 138 = _____

Multiply these.

7. 73 × 16 = _____
8. 39 × 25 = _____
9. 54 × 36 = _____

10. Circle the division that has a remainder of 2.

    378 ÷ 7   615 ÷ 9   450 ÷ 8   381 ÷ 4

11–12. Which two factors of 42 have a total of 17? _____ and _____

13. What is the smallest number that is a common multiple of 9 and 4?

    _____

14. What is the smallest number that is a common multiple of 8 and 6?

    _____

Complete the missing percentage, decimals and fraction in this conversion chart, giving the fraction in its lowest terms.

15–18

Fraction	$\frac{3}{10}$	$\frac{7}{100}$	$\frac{2}{5}$	$\frac{\Box}{\Box}$
Decimal	0.3	0.07	0.____	0.____
Percentage	30%	____%	40%	80%

Write the next number in each sequence.

19 1.5   3   4.5   6   ____

20 $\frac{1}{4}$ $\frac{3}{4}$ $1\frac{1}{4}$ $1\frac{3}{4}$ ____

21 0.7   0.9   1.1   1.3   ____

22 10.5   8   5.5   3   ____

Look at this pattern that has been made from colouring squares on a grid.

In this pattern a 'ring' of squares is shaded around the centre square, which is blank.

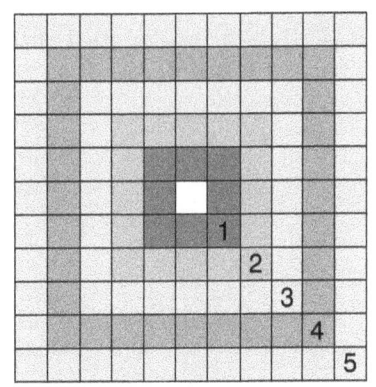

23–24 This table shows the number of squares shaded in each ring. Write the number of squares that have been shaded on the 4th and 5th ring of this sequence.

Ring (r)	1	2	3	4	5
Squares (s)	8	16	24	____	____

25 Circle the correct formula for this pattern.

   $8 - r = s$ $8r = s$ $8 + r = s$ $8 \div r = s$

26 How many squares will be shaded in the 10th ring? ____

27 What shape will be made when this net is folded?

_____

28 When this net is folded, how many vertices will this shape have?

_____ vertices

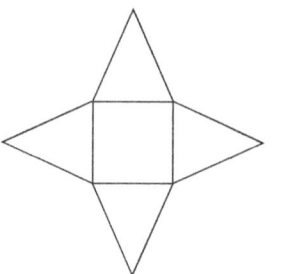

29 Complete this sentence with one of the following:

always, **sometimes**, **never**

An isosceles triangle _____ has a right angle.

30 Calculate the size of angle x in this isosceles triangle. Angle x = ___°

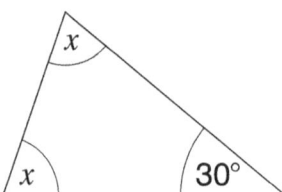

This is the plan of a house in a garden.

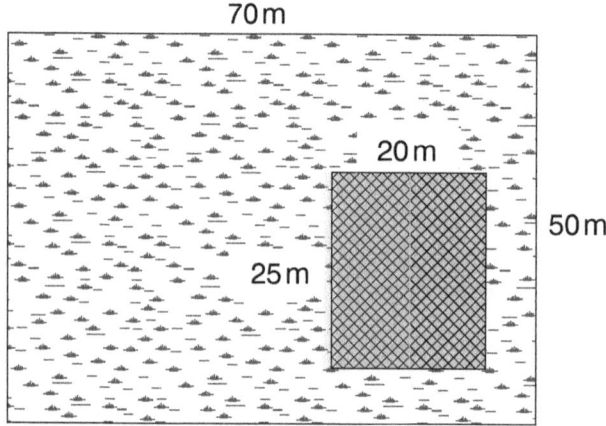

31 What is the area of the house? _____ m²

32 What is the area of the garden, not including the area of the house?

_____ m²

33 What is the perimeter of the house? _____ m

34 What is the perimeter of the garden? _____ m

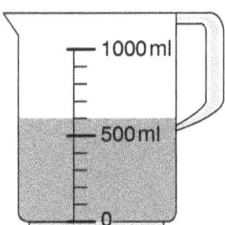
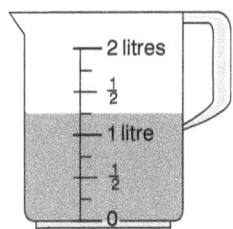

35 What is the difference between the amount of water in these two jugs?

_____ ml

36 What is the total amount of water in these two jugs? _____ litres

37 Write <, > or = to make this statement true.

350 g ___ 3.5 kg

38 A brick is 30 cm long. How many bricks will there be in one row of a wall that is 3 m long? _____

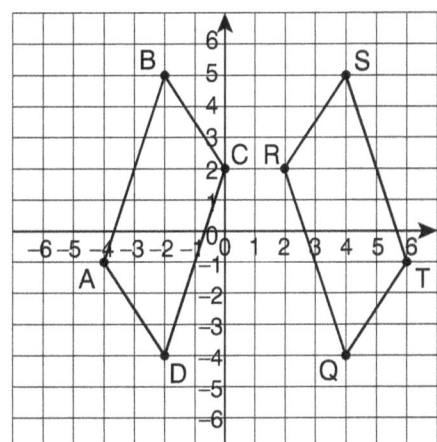

Draw a line to match each point with its coordinates.

39–41 Position A   Position C   Position T

(−2, 5)   (0, 2)   (4, −4)

(−4, −1)   (6, −1)   (−2, −4)

42 Complete this sentence with **translation**, **rotation** or **reflection**.

Parallelogram QRST is a _____ of parallelogram ABCD.

This graph shows the distance and time of Hannah's 10 km sponsored walk.

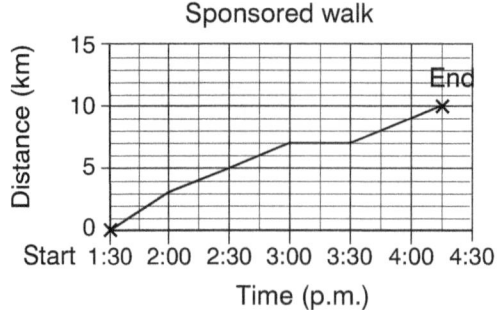

43 How many kilometres had Hannah walked by 2 o'clock? _____

44 How far did Hannah walk between 2:00 and 2:30? _____

45 Hannah had a half hour rest during the walk. Underline the correct time of Hannah's rest.

      1:30–2:00 p.m.   2:00–2:30 p.m.   2:30–3:00 p.m.
      3:00–3:30 p.m.   3:30–4:00 p.m.

46 Approximately what time did Hannah finish the 10 km walk? _____

These are digit cards 1–12. All the cards are shuffled and one card is picked out at random each time and then replaced.

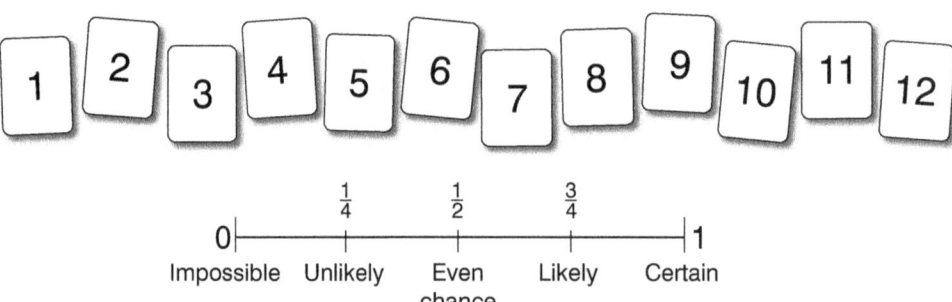

What is the likelihood of picking these? Write your answer as a fraction.

    47 What is the likelihood of picking an even number? _____

    48 What is the likelihood of picking a multiple of 4? _____

    49 What is the likelihood of picking a 1-digit number? _____

    50 Circle the likelihood of picking the number 13.

        0   50 : 50   1

Now go to the Progress Chart to record your score!   Total